The
GIFT OF
TIME

WILLIAM T. McCONNELL

INTER-VARSITY PRESS
DOWNERS GROVE
ILLINOIS 60515

נח

© 1983 by Inter-Varsity Christian Fellowship of the United States of America

InterVarsity Press is the book-publishing division of Inter-Varsity Christian Fellowship, a student movement active on campus at hundreds of universities, colleges and schools of nursing. For information about local and regional activities, write IVCF, 233 Langdon St., Madison, WI 53703.

Distributed in Canada through InterVarsity Press, 860 Denison St., Unit 3, Markham, Ontario L3R 4H1 Canada.

All quotations from Scripture, unless otherwise noted, are taken from the Holy Bible: New International Version. Copyright © 1978 by the New York International Bible Society. Used by permission of Zondervan Bible Publishers.

Luci Shaw's poem on p. 21 is reprinted from The Secret Trees *by Luci Shaw by permission of Harold Shaw Publishers. Copyright © 1976 by Luci Shaw.*

"Time, Gentlemen, Please" on p. 52 is used by permission of David J. Blow. Copyright © Subverse 1959.

The poem by Ada Lum on p. 79 is reprinted by permission from HIS, student magazine of Inter-Varsity Christian Fellowship, © 1979.

Michael Quoist's poem on p. 91 is taken from Prayers. *Copyright, 1963, Sheed and Ward, Inc. Reprinted with permission of Andrews and McMeel, Inc. All rights reserved.*

Cover illustration: Roberta Polfus

ISBN 0-87784-838-6

Printed in the United States of America

Library of Congress Cataloging in Publication Data

McConnell, William T., 1941-
    The gift of time.

    Bibliography: p.
    1. Time (Theology)   I. Title.
BT78.M393   1983   248.4   83-120
ISBN 0-87784-838-6

18 17 16 15 14 13 12 11 10 9 8 7 6 5 4 3 2 1
95 94 93 92 91 90 89 88 87 86 85 84 83

To my children:
Bill, who paces himself,
Janie, who goes full-steam every second she's awake,
and Debora, who weaves time into a poem.

Foreword

Christian life and thought are enriched today by the flow of people, cultures and ideas within the fellowship of God's worldwide family. McConnell's book is an excellent expression of this enriching process. You will find it not only easy to read but delightful. More than that, you will be challenged toward more maturity and fulfillment in the use of a gift you no doubt have: the gift of time.

Bill McConnell and his family are Americans who serve God in Brazil. They are part of the staff of the Aliança Bíblica Universitária, an indigenous evangelical student movement there. In his style and type of ministry Bill exemplifies "partnership in mission," the only viable approach for future missionary work on our planet. Do not be deceived by the easy flow of his style. Behind it there is serious theological work: Bill is "doing theology" at its best.

Missionary experience and praxis led Bill to question the validity of some of his assumptions about time and management. As he started to revise his American presuppositions in light of his Latin American experience, he had to reach back to the depths of biblical teaching. His acquaintance with church history provided another avenue of understanding. This tour through deeper sources helped him to find new ways of obeying God in his relation to time, that unique and universal gift. As he shares his experience in this book, he gives us not only an intellectual exercise but also much needed practical direction and help. Thus his theological work becomes pastoral.

We thank God for Bill's ministry in Latin America. As an organized brother with a disciplined commitment to Christ, he has taught many of us how to make the best use of our time. And he has done it with love and a good touch of humor. I am glad he has taken time to write this book. Having read it, I will not be the same. Neither will you, I hope.

Lima
November 1982
Samuel Escobar
IFES Associate General Secretary for Latin America

Preface

Shortly after arriving in Brazil, I attended a promotional dinner for the Brazilian equivalent of Inter-Varsity Christian Fellowship, the Aliança Bíblica Universitária. The meal was served one hour late. As the minutes after 6:10 crawled past, my stomach twisted into an ever tighter knot. I was sure that everyone would become disgusted and leave.

Nothing of the sort happened. People were enjoying themselves with friends they hadn't seen in years. They took time to look over the book table and the photograph display. No one looked anxiously at the clock. I was the only one up tight.

No, not the only one. The M.C. was a bit concerned because the speaker did not show up. A phone call revealed that he was still at home: a friend seeking counsel had arrived from out of town. Certainly one troubled sheep was more important than the 399 already corralled? Yes, of course. So the M.C. asked a well-known pastor who was still waiting for his dinner to fill in. The warmth and grace of his acceptance was matched by that of his message.

Such was my initiation to a culture of improvisation, a way of life that views schedules and programs quite differently from what I had experienced in a "prepackaged" society. I had never realized how unorganized I was until I joined a North American evangelical organization; I had not realized how inflexible I was until I became a missionary.

This book grew out of a course I taught on self-management at the Baptist Theological Seminary in São Paulo, Brazil. As I began to put together my thoughts and observations concerning time and ministry, I came across a newly translated book dealing with time management for Christians. It contained many helpful suggestions, in spite of its slightly North American flavor. But what disturbed me was the author's biblical justification for efficiency and time saving. The argument was based on the phrase "redeeming the time" from Colossians 4:5 and Ephesians 5:16. The exposition, which would have been accepted without comment in the United States, looked distorted in a different context. Could it be that our view of time and redemption had become warped through a watch crystal? Was time made for man, or man for time? I am grateful to my students for the insights and pointers which stimulated this organization of our discoveries.

I appreciate, too, the gift of time from Marvin Mayers, who read the manuscript and offered thoughtful comments and suggestions. Whether I learned enough from him to redeem this book, time will tell. I am delighted that my friend and colleague Samuel Escobar agreed to write the foreword.

My thanks must also be extended to Natalie Vasquez and Joanna Sparks, whose library skills made research over vast distances not only possible but also enjoyable and efficient. And to my wife, who kept her mother waiting while she finished making corrections in the final draft, I extend the thanks of Lemuel: "Her works bring her praise at the city gate."

Part 1.
Time,
Personality
and Culture

1. The Time of Your Life

Time is so pervasive, such an ubiquitous factor, that it is as ignored as one might suppose a goldfish ignores water.
JERRY FRYE, TIME: A SIGNIFICANT VARIABLE

The gods confound the man who first found out
How to distinguish hours—confound him, too,
Who in this place set up a sun-dial
To cut and hack my days so wretchedly
Into small pieces!
PLAUTUS, ROME, SECOND CENTURY B.C.

The silent clock, if consulted, agrees. "You may"; the chiming clock gently remarks "you should"; but the alarm shrills out insistently "you must!"
LAWRENCE WRIGHT, CLOCKWORK MAN

In the beginning God created the heavens and the earth" (Gen 1:1). In so doing, God also created time. Long before Einstein and the theory of relativity, Augustine reasoned, "How could those countless ages have elapsed when you, the Creator, in whom all ages have their origin, had not yet created them? What time could there have been that was not created by you? How could time elapse if it never was?"[1]

The ancient Hebrews early recognized the day, month and year as means of dividing or measuring time because these measurements involved the circuit of the earth, moon and sun.[2] They also observed the seven-day week, for which there is no satisfactory explanation except for divine revelation.[3] The day was divided into several parts, such as the "Watch" (Ex 14: 24; Judg 7:19; Ps 63:6), but there was no concern with lesser divisions such as the hour, minute and second.

Later, the development of the sundial, known in the reigns of kings Ahaz and Hezekiah (2 Kings 20:10-11; Is 38:8) permitted more exact measurements. Certainly by New Testament times monetary value was attached to the hours of the day (Mt 20:10-11).

But respect for time jumped dramatically in the eighth century when Pope Paul I gave to Pepin the Short, king of the Franks, a water clock that operated an alarm.[4] The clock, created to help us control our time, could now control us.

The clock measures . . . what? The passage of our lives. The ticking away of hours and minutes (or, if we have gone digital, the blinking away of seconds) represents the passing of part of our lives, and we feel pressured to do more with time: not just to be busier, but to accomplish something. Robert Schuller has turned this pressure into his life philosophy: "I began my lifework on the assumption that I might not live long enough to accomplish everything I'd like to. If I wanted to do anything worthwhile in my life I'd have to hurry up. I have been in a hurry ever since."[5]

Other people in a hurry have found time to write—and read— countless books on how to accomplish more in the same twenty-four hours allotted to us all, but often carelessly squandered. Written for practical people, the titles go straight to the point: *How to Get More Done in Less Time, The Management of Time, How to Get Control of Your Time and Your Life,* and *Time: How to Squeeze the Most Out of It.* Christians, too, have joined the rush to do something before it is too late, following time managers who basically apply principles from the field of business administration to the Christian's personal and church activities. These are serious books, well worth our time.

But not everyone has accepted the goals of time management and efficiency so seriously. Most of us can say *rat race* and *deadline* without the trace of a smile, but some people who have made their peace with the time clock ease the pressure on all of us with their lighthearted jibes at the Establishment. Erma Bombeck, for example, has undoubtedly saved the sanity of many a time-pressed homemaker with her witty anecdotes on the blessed disorderliness of our lives. On saving time she writes, "I used to spend hours hiding things I valued so the kids wouldn't find them, and then use up precious time trying to find them myself. Now I simply put anything I don't want to be discovered under the dish towel. In 28 years, no one has ever touched it but me." And for dealing with the business world she offers this advice: "Balancing checkbooks was always such a time-consuming chore until one day I discovered you could open up an account in a brand new bank in 10 minutes: four days less than it took to balance your old checkbook."[6]

What less-than-organized person, harassed by punctual colleagues, would not raise a cheer for Les Waas, president of the Procrastinators Club of America, when he says, "People who rush around and never relax and get all worried about being on time are people who die early. Then they are referred to as the 'late Mr. so-and-so.' Why not be late while you're alive? . . . It's surprising how many problems become less important, or even disappear, if you postpone them."[7] We can be sure that an organization whose slogan is "Procrastinate now" will not solve any problems of time pressure, at least not right away. And, as tempting as it may seem to laugh off the breathless pace of modern life, or dream of returning to a less hurried age, the only real hope of a solution to time pressure lies in coming to terms with the time we have.

We have all noticed that sometimes time flies, sometimes it drags, and other times it just lies there heavy on our hands. That is, our inner time responds differently to the steady pace of the clock, depending on what is happening within and around us. We all know the frustration of being into something and then finding that time is up, as the British playwright J. B. Priestley describes: "As soon as we make full use of our faculties, commit ourselves heart and soul to anything, live richly and intensely, instead of merely existing, our inner-time spends our ration of clock-time as a drunken sailor his pay."[8]

The solution? We could try to stretch our clock time by not committing ourselves to anything, says Priestley, spending "yawning hours with boring and mechanical people or dreary little pursuits." Or we might do what businessmen do: "appoint a kind of policeman from outer time to control the antics and vagaries of our inner time." But he quickly dismisses that idea, too: "When one of these important and successful men awards us 15 minutes of his outer time, we can often see that policeman in his eyes, hear him in the guarded voice. But although this control of inner time might bring more success and importance, few of us feel it would enrich experience or make for a good life."[9]

Just what is this good life to which we can commit ourselves without regret or misgivings? Can it really be what Wall Street and Madison Avenue hold out to us, the American way of life? I share the cynicism of Peter Cohen, a graduate of the Harvard Business School, when he defines the American creed as

> That outworn, hilariously twisted and disfigured ethic which urges people to compete for the sake of competing, achieve for the sake of achieving, win for the sake of winning, and which honors him who does all this without pause or let-up—the fastest, the richest, the smartest, the nicest, the sportiest, the artiest; because things wouldn't be the way they are unless God meant them to be.[10]

As Cohen recognizes, America has its civil religion. Its God is progress and its ethic consists of hard work and competition. Its founders include Thomas Jefferson and Benjamin Franklin, deists who used biblical language to describe the new democratic experiment. For them, the kingdom of God was being established in the wilderness of North America, and the chosen people were those who built this new temporal paradise.

Franklin inspired the chosen people to be thrifty and disciplined with their time, and he is still a favorite source of quotations by time-management moralists. "Dost thou love life? Then do not squander time, for that is the stuff life is made of."[11] Larry Rasmussen, in his recent study on America's economic tradition, comments, "The line that runs steadily from Benjamin Franklin to a thousand self-help groups today is the tradition of self-managed self-improvement."[12]

Religious pluralism has today blurred the distinction between Christianity and America's civil religion. Prosperity has made us defensive toward critical evaluation of the capitalist system. Andrew Kirk rightly says that "living standards measured in quantitative terms is the name of the game. Many Christians, in all honesty, are playing the game in deadly earnest, personally committed to its success, even when this may endanger our health and cause suffering to others, for we are literally and metaphorically up to our eyes in debt to the system."[13]

Jesus was not talking about "the American way" or "the good life," however, when he spoke of "the way, the truth and the life." Neither is it fair to pin a "made in USA" label on the kingdom of God. Certainly the God of the Bible cannot be blamed for whatever "virtues" have become euphemisms for the greed, status and power which seem to motivate our inalienable right to pursue happiness. God's kingdom comes; it is not spread like a disease or set up like a committee. Jesus urged people to enter the kingdom, not build it.

If Christians in the United States must not breathlessly pursue the American Dream, it is not because of cynicism for the present or hopelessness for the future. Nor are we cultural iconoclasts; there is no need per se to get rid of the human to make room for the divine. No, the problem with the American way is not human culture itself nor the "gigantic laboratory for the experiment of modernization," as Peter Berger calls the United States,[14] but rather Satan's grip on them. God has broken that grip, and this is what gives our efforts hope and meaning. As we look to God's ultimate victory at the end of time, we temper the urgency of our service with patience; we wait to see how he will fulfill his plan (Rom 8:22-25).

Didn't Jesus say that we were to be busy about our Father's business? No, he didn't. (If the "verse" sounds familiar, compare Luke 2:49.) Jesus, like other men, had work to do, but the Gospels do not reveal him as rushed or anxious over the passing of time. What Jesus did was not done with an airline timetable in his hand. Oh, that his followers would exhibit the same sense of purpose and calm! What Eugene Peterson says of linking the word *busy* with *pastor* should apply to all Christians. "The word *busy* is the symptom not of commitment, but of betrayal. It is not devotion but defection. The adjective *busy* set as a modifier to *pastor* should sound to our ears like *adulterous* to characterize a wife, or *embezzling* to describe a banker. It is an outrageous scandal, a blasphemous affront."[15]

"But," we sputter, "Christians must not be lazy!" Of course not. But busy and lazy are false alternatives. To see the options this way only indicates that we have not yet grasped the full impact of the Fall on our commitments and time, nor yet perceived how much God's redeeming us changes our relation to time. "The days are evil"; that is, both time itself and our experience of it must know God's redemptive power.

It may seem simplistic, even mystical, to propose that our hope lies in our devotional life. But if, as C. S. Lewis so aptly illustrates in *The Great Divorce,* the gates of hell are bolted from the inside, then only an inner transformation can meet the purpose. God's re-creation begins within our inner time, releasing the pressure on the mainspring of our lives. With eternity in our hearts, there is no need to be harassed in our schedules. "In repentance and rest is your salvation, in quietness and trust is your strength" (Is 30:15).

Can the church keep its composure as the world rushes by, calling it to "keep up with the times"? Only if it remembers that it is preparing to be a bride, and not a bank manager or a policeman. Time spent with the Beloved means something altogether different from time spent with the rest of the crowd.

2. Time and Temperament

What is time? The shadow on the dial, the striking of the clock, the running of the sand, day and night, summer and winter, months, years, centuries—these are but arbitrary and outward signs, the measure of Time, not Time itself. Time is the Life of the soul.
HENRY WADSWORTH LONGFELLOW, HYPERION

Time may be mysterious, but it also possesses an admirable objective purity, a sort of narrative genius, like Tolstoy. But what is a civilization to do when it discovers that time also thinks like James Joyce, or worse?
LANCE MORROW, TIME *MAGAZINE*

Man cannot
name himself.

He waits for God
or Satan
to tell him
who he is.
LUCI SHAW, THE SECRET TREES

A person's view of time is a method of discerning his personality. . . . Tell me what you think of time and I shall know what to think of you." These words do not come from a business executive interviewing someone for a job or from a psychology textbook. They come from a philosopher, J. T. Fraser, in his introduction to a superb study on the philosophy of time.[1] But even if he is not concerned about hiring or psychoanalyzing someone, Fraser is certainly doing more than philosophizing. Both the business executive and the social scientist would agree with his statement, but for different reasons.

For people in management, time is a commodity to be used, to be manipulated. Jim Davidson, author of *Effective Time Management,* writes, "Time is an invaluable resource. When time is not utilized effectively, productivity and money are automatically lost. How you arrange your time is how you arrange your life and in your business, managing time is often synonymous with managing the job."[2] Richard Bolles, an Episcopal priest helping people with their philosophy of work, has helped prospective employees to see that their use of time is a self-management skill, one that is not only learned but also marketable.[3] The ability to plan, keep appointments and do more in less time will certainly affect how your boss thinks of you.

To refer to time as a resource and our use of it as a skill already reveals a thought pattern or value commitment; it suggests a personal interpretation of what is happening "out there." We must recognize time "out there" and the importance of stewardship of it as part of the creation over which humanity has dominion. But we must also value " inner time," the internal rhythm which measures the value of events and not just their duration. Time is not just external change, but also our very life, and how we use it reveals who we are. The introvert and the extrovert, for example, operate on different inner clocks. That is, by the very nature of their personalities they relate differently to the outward measure of time. J. B. Priestley tells us a lot about himself (and us) when he writes, "Clocktime is our bank manager, tax collector, police inspector; inner-time is our wife."[4]

Of course, bank managers, tax collectors and police inspectors are important people. We are grateful for them and respect them. But a wife or husband is different. When we return home from having dealt with these serious and unforgiving defenders of society, we are glad for the embrace of someone who loves us for who we are and offers us something totally different from what bank managers, tax collectors and the police offer. And why is it that the moments with our spouse seem to pass so much more quickly than the hours we spend trying to get a loan or filling out tax forms?

To admit at the start that the philosophical and scientific problems of time are not my concern undoubtedly tells Dr. Fraser a great deal about me. It is not that I think objective, chronological time unimportant, but only that the mere passage of time-in-itself (if there can be such a thing) does not give us the answers that we search for. What does the passage of time *mean?* I contend that spouses tell us more about that than do bank managers, tax collectors or the police.

Our industrial society with its increasingly technological precision is putting a strain on the relationship between our inner perception of time and the chronological time that we are becoming so good at measuring. Jet lag, for example, is a symptom of our inner clock's being out of phase with the external clock. Executive "burn-out" may be another symptom of a time-related disease affecting not just a person's body and mind, but his or her very being. The pace of our age threatens us all with schizophrenia, a divorce of inner time from human personality.[5]

Time and Personality

We begin, then, not with the study of moments "out there," but rather with the people who perceive them pass by and the ways they divide, classify and interpret the external changes we call time. Are you inner-directed? Other-directed? An introvert? An extrovert? An Oriental? A European? Our perception of time depends on many personal and cultural traits called temperaments or, sometimes, personality types. Numerous category systems have been developed, variously called cognitive styles, learning grids, communication styles and so on. The idea of temperaments, especially as elaborated by Carl Jung and Ole Hallesby, can help Christians to understand themselves both in relation to other people and also to time. The study of these traits has a long history.

The division of personality into four main categories comes from the ancient medical belief that the body contained four fluids: blood, phlegm, choler (or yellow bile) and melancholy (or black bile). The differences in people's temperaments depended on how these four "humors" were blended in the body. If the blood predominated, the person was said to be *sanguine,* exhibiting a warm, lively personality, given to the moment. The phlegmatic, with a richer blend of phlegm, would be cool, slow, more detached from the press of events. The choleric person would be hot-blooded, eager, oriented toward the future. If melancholy were dominant, the person would be serious, dark, even gloomy, given to meditation on the past.

Of course, this physical basis for temperament has long been abandoned; but the concept of temperaments has continued, and the four categories are still useful. Jung in his book *Psychological Types,* published in 1923, updated the terminology, substituting "sensation type" for the sanguine, "thinking type" for the phlegmatic, "intuitive type" for the choleric and "feeling type" for the melancholic. But the classical names too have retained their popularity, especially since the publication of *Temperament and the Christian Faith* by Ole Hallesby and, more recently, the study on the Psychotypology of Time," which appeared in *The Future of Time* in· 1971.[6]

To divide personality into only four types is not only an oversimplification, but it is also a threat to many people. No one likes to be categorized that simply. In reality, of course, temperaments are never found "pure" in any individual, group or society. Subtypes abound. Above all, our God is infinitely creative and has no need to mass-produce human personality. Each person is a "limited edition," and no attempt to generalize must efface God's individual mark of uniqueness.

Even so, general categories can be useful. Just as we think of national, linguistic or social categories, we can distinguish among general characteristics of temperament whether in an individual or in a culture. When we say that a person is choleric, for example, or has a choleric temperament, we mean only that his energetic, future-oriented personality predominates in the blending of traits.

Complete descriptions of the various personality traits and of some subtypes are available elsewhere.[7] We will concern ourselves only with these traits as they reflect an orientation toward time. Hallesby establishes this link: "Temperament has to do only with the functioning of the soul-life. It strikes the key or chord to which the soul must vibrate. It gives the *tempo* which will control the natural *rhythm* of soul and body" (emphasis mine).[8]

In daily life we see this expressed in simple descriptions of the way people relate to their work, their leisure and other people:

"She always seems to have time for everything."

"He sure knows how to have a good time."

"She takes such a long time to do anything."

"His time is so precious."

These phrases express a dominant trait, a perhaps unconscious view of time which becomes a clue to understanding personality.

One caution: *Temperament* does not determine character. Is an outgoing, present-oriented sanguine person more moral or spiritual than a detached, reflective phlegmatic? I think not. Each temperament includes patterns of reactions that may become virtues like kindness, patience or joy. But each also includes a bent to some vice or sin which we as Christians must fight: sloth, impatience, uncaringness and so on. No one temperament is closer to being "conformed to the image of his Son" than any other (Rom 8:29 RSV).

All people need to be redeemed, no matter how socially acceptable their natural traits. There are no naturally sanctified personalities, just as there are no unredeemable ones. What we have and what we are are gifts which can either be dedicated to their Giver or ungratefully squandered in self-indulgence.

When we look at the weaknesses inherent in our temperaments, we may be tempted to identify them with the "unregenerate man." But when we examine the positive aspects of our natural temperaments, we see them as gifts, a part of the image of God reflected in us. Our temperaments, then, like our wills or emotions, suffer the effects of the Fall and must be constantly redeemed and dedicated to their Lord and Creator. It should not be surprising that as God gains control of us, we will gain control over the time he has given us.

In many cases a conversion experience brings immediate and radical changes in a person's basic outlook on life. His temperament appears to change overnight. For others the process of change is not so dramatic. If you are an extrovert, you will not stop being outgoing; but you will become easier to live with. If you are basically an introvert, you will not suddenly cease being shy. But it will become easier for you to live with yourself. No matter what your basic temperament, once it is being molded by the Holy Spirit you will find opportunities for service, and the gift aspect of your personality will emerge and flourish.

In this process of discovering ourselves, of perceiving our more obvious personality traits, we may feel judged by them (as in the one-sentence descriptions of people above), or we may become critical of the slow progress of others. In either case, we must remember Jesus' warning to deal with the splinter in our own eyes first. It is easy to excuse ourselves ("We cholerics are all hard headed") or to label others ("You melancholics are so gloomy"). Instead, we are to let our "minds be remade and [our] whole nature thus transformed" (Rom 12:2 NEB).

Part of this renewing of our mind involves changing how we view the time we call ours, for it is not really ours at all. C. S. Lewis shows us how unreasonably jealous we are of our daily allotment of hours in Screwtape's advice to the junior tempter, Wormwood. Wormwood is to tempt his subject to "zealously guard in his mind the curious assumption 'My time is my own.' " But he warns, "You have here a delicate task. The assumption which you want him to go on making is so absurd that, if once it is questioned, even we cannot find a shred of argument in its defence. The man can neither make, nor retain, one moment of time; it all comes to him by pure gift; he might as well regard the sun and moon as his chattels."⁹

Cultural Traits

When a whole group of people exhibit the same rhythm of life, these classifications can apply to an entire society or culture.¹⁰ Easterners or urban Midwesterners, for example, feel the difference when they visit the South or the West Coast. A Chicagoan who visited friends in Texas recently commented, "I couldn't stand to live there. They don't take time as seriously as we do."

Anyone who has traveled abroad has experienced this difference of tempo. In a hundred humorous (or frustrating) ways he senses a different attitude toward history, change and the future. What diplomat or businessman has not discovered that it takes longer to accomplish anything in Southeast Asia? Or how many times has a missionary in Latin America tried to begin a meeting on time, only to discover that he was the only one present? Rudyard Kipling reflected on this in the days of the British Empire:

> Now it is not good for the Christian's health
> to hustle the Aryan brown,
> For the Christian riles, and the Aryan smiles
> and he weareth the Christian down;
> And the end of the fight is a tombstone white
> with the name of the late deceased,
> And the epitaph drear: "A Fool lies here
> who tried to hustle the East."¹¹

The Latin temperament is basically sanguine. Consider the South American love for fiesta, the back-slapping *abrazos* when friends meet, the *mañana* view toward the future. The Latin is a personable, open, receptive person, given to the moment. For the Latin, time is love to be shared liberally with friends or offered generously to those in need. He or she enjoys the relational portions of the Bible, especially the Psalms and the Gospels. Who more than a Latin responds so emotionally to the story of Mary anointing Jesus' feet? And the Latin regards the North American, in contrast, as banal, rigid and dull.

The African theologian John Mbiti suggests that traditional African society may be basically melancholic. For the Akamba and other traditional societies he knows, history moves "backwards." It is the past which is important, not the future.[12] A powerful instance showing the value placed on history and tradition occurs in Alex Haley's *Roots*. When Haley visited the area of Africa from which his ancestor had been captured by slavers, he listened to the African *griot* recount the significant events in the life of the tribe, from memory, back to the point at which his ancestor was mentioned. Such tradition-oriented societies usually have little concern for the future or for haste, unlike Haley's North American colleagues.

When people from another culture step into North America, they immediately feel a different pulse-beat. A university student, reared by missionary parents in Africa, wrote that when he came to the United States to study, "everything seemed to blare out; do, taste, experience, buy, absorb, read, feel, be—and *quick*, before it's too late."[13] Some observers, such as the Brazilian sociologist Vianna Moog, can hardly contain their disdain for the North American pace of life: "The American no longer knows how to contemplate; he does not know how to reflect or even rest."[14]

To be sure, the Anglo-Saxon temperament is predominantly that of the practical choleric. Here is a people which plans, decides, acts. What other society gives such respect to futurologists, or seriously invests in pork-belly futures? If these people honored saints, Martha would certainly be favored over Mary as their patron. Inherent in their view that the future is coming in as planned seems to be the judgment that other cultures are impractical, sentimental and incapable of making progress.

It often surprises people brought up in choleric North

America to discover that much of their problem getting along in a different culture, whether just a few blocks or another continent away, comes from their basic attitude toward people with other temperaments. William Fawcett, pastor of Metropolitan Chapel in São Paulo, Brazil, has helped many business people and missionaries by explaining how the four psychological types adjust in cultural adaptation. Commented one executive's wife, "So that's why my husband is less tense now. He's very sanguine and he's finally working in a culture which understands him." An efficient, choleric-type missionary leader did not find life easier after the course, but she was able to locate the source of the conflict: "I can now understand why I get so furious over delays or things breaking down. It isn't just my plans, but me that's threatened."

Are such generalizations fair? Certainly these broad characterizations leave ample room for exceptions. But it is easy to test the broad sketches painted above. Just read the appropriate paragraphs to a group of Latins and then to a group of North Americans. Note the quizzical expressions and measured response of the North Americans, and the smiles and laughter of their southern neighbors.

The Japanese call the more expansive Latin or Filipino temperament "wet," while they would describe the typical Anglo-Saxon as "dry." Such generalizations can be applied to one individual's ability in relating to other people, or to describe the culture as a whole. The image is excellent to illustrate the reactions of people who are outside their normal milieu. How do dry people respond when placed in a wet culture? Either they absorb some of the surrounding ethos and become a bit moist themselves, or they remain a small island in what to them is a damp and perhaps unwholesome place. Conversely, someone from a wet culture will feel like a drop of water on a soda cracker unless he or she is willing to penetrate the crust of the environment.

The analogy is limited, of course, for certainly we do not want to conclude that the ideal solution to intercultural misunderstandings and differences is a kind of damp mush in which cultural distinctions have been diluted to a bland uniformity. Instead, the goal is to understand our own culture, which we so rarely see objectively. To do this, some comparisons with other cultures are helpful. By noticing carefully what happens to us when we encounter a different concept of time and by withholding judgment temporarily, we can learn something about our own perception of time. In the process we may discover values in other cultures which we have overlooked because of the limitations of our perception.

3. Telling Time in Tijuana

Leisure is still a monstrous puzzle for everyone nurtured
on the Protestant ethic.
EUGENE C. KENNEDY, A TIME FOR LOVE

There is a slowness in affairs that ripens them, and a slowness
which rots them.
JOSEPH ROUX, MEDITATIONS OF A PARISH PRIEST

Rabbits, of course, have no idea of precise time or of punctuality. In
this respect they are much the same as primitive people, who
often take several days over assembling for some purpose and then several
more to get started.
RICHARD ADAMS, WATERSHIP DOWN

José de Alencar, the Brazilian novelist of the last century, entitled one of his best-known romances *Five Minutes*. The title comes from the beginning of the story where the principal character misses his bus by just five minutes because of his habit of always being late. On the later bus he meets his future wife, and so he considers his destiny happily determined by his not having the "bad habit of the English," punctuality.[1]

Undoubtedly, the English—and the Swiss and the Germans, to add only a few—would not think of punctuality as a bad habit; it is a virtue, or at least a common courtesy. North Americans, along with all those peoples who have experienced the industrial revolution, have a strong choleric sense of the value of time. The French are perhaps more choleric-sanguine, the Japanese more choleric-phlegmatic; but wherever the business virtues of exactness, precision and punctuality are cultivated with a relish, there you will find what has been called a time-oriented culture.² To avoid confusion, since all the temperaments and all cultures are time-oriented in one way or another, I will use Daniel Bell's term *future-oriented* to describe the Western, choleric-dominated temperament. Speaking of the United States as representative of all future-oriented societies, he says that American society no longer grows naturally; instead, it must be "mobilized for specific ends."³ And it is easiest to mobilize a person toward a distant goal when "being on time" has become a good habit.

In contrast to the West are event-oriented cultures where the more emotive temperaments tend to dominate. These cultures measure time by the sequence of significant events rather than by uniform divisions of clock time. John Mbiti explains sympahetically the traditional time-reckoning pattern in Africa:

> Time reckoning according to the Akamba (and other African societies) is governed by phenomena rather than mathematics. People reckon time for a concrete and specific purpose: one event in relation to another. . . . It does not matter whether the month is 25 or 35 days long, or whether the year is 330 or 380 days long. So long as the events that constitute a complete month or year take place, then the month or year is complete, since it is the events and not the mathematics which constitute time and hence determine its reckoning.⁴

Such experience-oriented societies are more sanguine (or sanguine-melancholic), focusing on the importance of the moment and the sense of completeness inherent in the event taking place. People in event-oriented societies are "interested in who's there, what's going on, and how one can embellish the event with sound, color, light, body movement, touch, etc. [They are] less interested in time and schedule."[5] Try to buy an airplane ticket in Latin America while one of the ticket agents is telling a story to the others, and you will sense this acutely!

Marvin Mayers has summarized the differences of outlook between the event-oriented and the future-oriented people. The event-oriented person:

☐ is not too concerned with time periods,

☐ will bring people together without planning a detailed schedule and see what develops,

☐ will work over a problem or idea until resolved or exhausted, regardless of time,

☐ lives in the here-and-now and does not plan a detailed schedule for the future,

☐ is not much concerned with history, and

☐ trusts in his own experience, while is careful about accepting another's experience.

Mayers notes that the future-oriented person, on the other hand,

☐ sets time periods for accomplishing tasks, depending on the intent or purpose of the time spent,

☐ plans the time period carefully, in order to accomplish the most possible in the time allotted,

☐ is alert to the "range of punctuality" at the beginning and end of the time period,

☐ sets goals, plans ahead,

☐ is likely to assign a time/dollar equivalence, or a time spent/production equivalence,

☐ will not fear the unknown too greatly, and

☐ will remember and try to reinforce times and dates.[6]

It is easy to see that the United States is in the future-oriented camp, although there are sizable minorities, such as Hispanics and Indians, which belong to the other camp. These minorities, and even individuals in the majority group, will chafe to the extent that their view of time conflicts with that of the majority. They will feel tension and experience constant misunderstanding if they do not conform to the time schedules which are so important to the majority choleric-type.

The potential for misunderstanding is illustrated by the mental images of time suggested in transcultural management surveys.[7] Highly motivated members of a future-oriented society choose an active metaphor for time, such as a galloping horseman, whereas event-oriented peoples less concerned with "achievement" are more likely to use for time the image of a deep, still ocean. Now imagine a horse trying to run through water: no wonder there are mutual frustrations when the two views meet!

Such images, however, create too great a contrast. In fact, no society is uniformly event- or future-oriented. There are always geographical regions or strata of society which feel the impact of the future more keenly than others. Rural, "interior" regions of each country are more prone to be event-oriented than the coastal cities or industrial areas. A student from a farm in Iowa told me that he takes off his watch when he goes home for the summer and puts it on again only when he returns to college in the fall. North Americans may view Latins as event-oriented, but to the indigenous peoples of South America the Latin is terribly time conscious.

It is better, then, to think of cultures and subcultures on a continuum. Those more self-contained, such as agricultural groups which govern their lives by the natural rhythm of the seasons, will be at one end; and the more interdependent, industrialized groups will cluster at the other end. Even within a dominantly choleric culture there will be a spectrum. Nevertheless, the closer we get to the split-second precision needed to measure sports events or to launch interplanetary rockets, the more we measure our lives by technical, time-telling equipment and the more likely we will hear the thundering hoofbeats of time in our souls.

Informal Patterns of Time

People easily become accustomed to the techniques of measuring time. Inexpensive wristwatches and pocket transistor radios have penetrated to places where even Coca-Cola is unknown. People who still measure time by the position of the sun are aware of political events on the other side of the world and know when to turn on the newscast. But to transfer the values of *internal* time patterns from one culture to another is a different story. How do you teach a group like the Sioux Indians, who have no word for *time,* or *late* or *waiting,* the values associated with being on time? Or how is an Anglo to know the importance of the occasion which he so unwittingly interrupted?

These internal patterns baffle those unfamiliar with them because they are not explicit or objective. You do not read them off a dial or hear them announced over the radio. Rather, they are implicit in the web of social contacts within a culture and can be perceived only by careful observation. Normally, in our own society, we take these patterns for granted because we were raised with them, and as Edward Hall suggests, they are not optional to the members of that society. We attach positive value to them. "They exist like the air around us. They are either familiar and comfortable, or unfamiliar and wrong."[8]

Wrong? Shouldn't we say "uncomfortable" (to keep the sentence parallel) or "strange"? In all fairness, yes, we should. To absolutize our informal idea of how late a person can be for an appointment or how late in the evening someone can telephone a friend without being rude is a form of ethnocentrism, an unwarranted pride in "our way of doing things." But in practice our first reaction is to judge that which is unfamiliar as wrong. In the same way that we can be critical of another person's basic personality make-up, we can write off the contributions of another culture without appreciating their positive values. "We do not ordinarily think of our way of behaving as being *one* way of behaving among others, but as *the* way to behave or act."[9]

Mere contact between cultures does not automatically bring about understanding. While traveling one summer with a group of university students in Europe, I was amazed to see that most of the students criticized or ridiculed all that made Europe unique and interesting. Rather than accept differences as just different, they became more entrenched in their own "right" way of doing things. We are all tempted to say with Guindon's isolationist cartoon figure, "Do you realize that with the exception of us, the world is made up of foreign countries?" In order to take the foreignness out of these contacts, we must be willing to relativize our own culture and desire to see what others consider important. The anthropologist Robert J. Maxwell relates one such mind-opening experience:

It is difficult perhaps for us to understand how unimportant time can become in a non-industrialized, non-Western setting. My watch stopped after the first few months of field work in Samoa and I found myself floating fluidly through the day, able only to make rough estimates of the time according to the position of the sun. I was hardly ever inconvenienced, and the experience itself was not entirely unpleasant.[10]

Event-oriented Work

Probably the aspect of an event-oriented society that is most criticized by Westerners is its view of work, which frustrates and baffles the future-oriented society. The West considers work as the means of making money; in most non-Western societies, work is more relational. Moog cites the Brazilian dictum, "Those who work don't have time to make money,"[11] reflecting the almost fatalistic idea that work really won't make much difference in one's lot in life. As Brazilians joke, "A Brazilian has two chances to get rich: when he is born and when he gets married." The best chances of success come from a strong network of family in influential places. Mayers has captured the seriousness of matrimonial alliances to this end: "The man stands to gain quite a bit by marriage. The prestige of a church wedding for him is equivalent to the North American college degree in its potential for opening doors of opportunity and establishing relationships with those who can be of social and economic aid."[12] Planning, saving and actively filling the time with work are not the best means to survival. Instead, the best way is to invest time in cultivating important relationships.

European and North American travelers in the so-called Third World often complain that the people do not want to "get ahead," that they have no sense of responsibility. Tourists fail to perceive that it is exactly because these event-oriented people do have a desire to improve their lot and do have a sense of responsibility that they do not meet the expectations of the more pragmatic future-oriented person. It was in this area of interpersonal relationships that the Peace Corps often encountered difficulties. In the more sanguine, event-oriented cultures people "develop long-lasting mutual assistance alliances based on reciprocal obligations, which often override personal consequences, and often "get in the way" of accomplishing specific technological or managerial tasks. Americans, by contrast, tend toward more short-range, impersonal contractual, functionally specific relationships."[13]

The story is told of Maria, who bought fruit from a wholesaler in the center of the city and then sold it house-to-house in the barrio. One regular customer, who usually bought only a few pieces of fruit, once offered to buy all she had for a family party. Maria refused, although the price would have been favorable. She explained that she could buy the fruit only early in the morning; if she sold all she had before noon, she would have nothing to offer her other customers, nothing to do the rest of the day and no news to tell her family that night.

The decision-making process in an event-oriented society is also strange to future-oriented business people. Many Latin organizations, both in Europe and South America, operate by consensus. One person who is not in full agreement with a proposal can delay action indefinitely. Consensus is not an efficient method. There is no vote to cut through disagreements; discussion may go on for hours over minor points. But consensus does foster fuller participation of all involved in whatever course of action is finally decided on.

Event-oriented managers work out details in general committee, keeping meetings going as long as necessary, whereas Anglo-Saxon, future-oriented administrators would delegate those details to a subcommittee for efficiency's sake. But the seemingly tedious method of the former insures that no one is deceived, that no suspicion arises and that business relationships remain harmonious. In experience-oriented cultures, time is not saved by using impersonal, efficient methods. Instead, time is invested in building human relationships. This type of management reflects the basic values of the sanguine-melancholic temperament, very different from the choleric values evident in North America.

Time in Church

In church life, too, the differences between future-oriented and experience-oriented views of time become important. The Christian faith looks back to God's work in history and also looks forward to the victorious end of history. In the present it calls for a moment-by-moment walk of faith. It is not hard to imagine that these time-related aspects of the message would appeal naturally to specific groups of people according to their time orientation. Should it be a surprise that predominantly choleric North America produces by far the most studies on eschatology? For traditional African societies, according to John Mbiti, the future holds no such fascination. He laments that missionary insensitivity to a fundamental difference between the African and Western concepts of time lies at the root of the proliferation of African church sects.[14]

Where missionaries and church leaders have been sensitive to these time-related social differences, the results beautifully satisfy the sense of completeness which experience-oriented peoples want. For example, Mariana Slocum and Florence Gerdel, Wycliffe Bible translators in southern Mexico, encouraged national expressions of worship in the newly formed church. One such expression was a worship service which would last three hours or more. Only the missionaries grew tired or bored. For the others, the meaning was not cut short by an arbitrary schedule.[15]

Or consider what kind of report should be given after an especially moving meeting or convention. When a Pentecostal pastor in Barquisimeto, Venezuela, reported on a recently held conference, he didn't reach for a sheaf of papers in his briefcase but instead picked up his guitar and sang a song.[16]

Cultural Dominance

Whenever two different world or time views meet, there is need for an adjustment, a re-education on the part of all involved, in order for each to understand the thought patterns of the others. Future-oriented and event-oriented cultures do not remain side by side without change indefinitely. They borrow from one another, but always very selectively.[17] In the case of an expanding industrial society, it is usually the event-oriented peoples who must make the major changes. The more "advanced" peoples trample the "quaint" practices of "backward" peoples in order to speed up so-called development.

Western society is not only triumphant; it is also triumphalistic. That is, it heralds its own victory as the obvious and best solution to cultural friction. Benjamin Franklin in 1757 noted this tendency in the Colonists' view of the Indians as savage because of their simpler lifestyle: "Savages we call them, because their manners differ from ours, which we think the perfection of civility; they think the same of theirs. . . . Our laborious manner of life, compared with theirs, they esteem slavish and base, and the learning on which we value ourselves, they regard as frivolous and useless."[18]

After two centuries there is still a "time problem" with the American Indians. Teachers and missionaries in the Southwest have emphasized the need to teach the Anglo time structure in grade school, to make the Indian bi-temporal as part of being bi-cultural. Only in this way can they maintain their own time structures but still catch the bus in the morning. It is the same everywhere: those coming in contact with Western society must learn to treat time technically if they hope to be considered normal and responsible.

Wherever Western powers have exercised economic or cultural dominance, time perception changes under cultural pressure. José de Alencar saw this process happening in the commercial classes of Brazil as that country began to meet the challenge of European industrialization. His romances showed the tension of traditional Brazilian society as it was forced into the mold of competition. The Brazilian literary critic Massaud Moisés, commenting on Alencar's famous novel *Senhora,* says that "the class to which Aurélia belonged, the bourgeoisie, became conformed to its image of time: ladylike, domesticated, well behaved, linear and inflexible."[19] The imperialist impulse has sought to control a people's every commitment, including their use of time.

Japanese theologian Kosuke Koyama attributes to this crusading, triumphalistic spirit the ineffectiveness of the Christian missionary effort in the Orient:

> Evangelism has not made any significant headway in Asia for the last 400 years because Christians crusaded against Asians. . . . I submit that a good hundred million American dollars, a hundred years of crusading will not make Asia Christian. Christian faith does not and cannot be spread by crusading. It will spread without money, without bishops, without theologians, without planning, if people see a crucified mind, not a crusading mind, in Christians.[20]

The effort to buy time or control it has its price. Peoples overwhelmed by an aggressive expansionism (whether geographical, economic or ideological) lose their basic self-concept as well as their cultural heritage. Deprivation and low self-esteem lead some to imitate the dominant culture, which usually means being cut off from their cultural roots. Others resist such a move and isolate themselves not only from the dominant choleric vision of the future, but also from those who are trying to bridge the gap. Anglos may praise those who have become integrated into the mainstream of society, but traditional Indians ridicule the "apple Indian" (red outside, white inside).

God's Timetable

It would be a mistake to think that these conflicts are insignificant, or to conclude that the sooner the Western view of time is adopted around the world, the better it will be for everybody. Just the opposite may be true. Even in what appears to impatient administrators of multinational companies as unnecessary delay and complications, there are positive values to be considered and respected. And in Christian missions, often the most rapid way to move forward is to go slowly.

To whatever extent we see time as a limited and decreasing resource ("time is money"), such an event-oriented philosophy does not make sense. But what if time is love? That is, what if the event-oriented culture is closer to how God intended us to relate to time? Koyama connects God's "speed" with his very nature (which is, of course, love and not mammon), and he suggests we are more likely to perceive him at work in our inner time rather than in the rush of activity:

God walks "slowly" because he is love. If he is not love he would have gone much faster. Love has its speed. It is an inner speed. . . . It is a different kind of speed from the technological speed to which we are accustomed. . . . It goes on in the depth of our life . . . at three miles an hour. It is the speed we walk and therefore it is the speed the love of God walks.[21]

If time is a love gift, something to be shared—to be invested, yes, but invested in people—could it be that we are missing something when we relate our time solely to efficiency and accomplishment? Does the choleric vision of time have a blind spot? Arthur Custance suggests that our frustration with the event-oriented view of time reflects a lack in our own discernment, a spiritual blindness to values which are being squeezed out of industrialized people:

> The sense of time is undoubtedly impressed most keenly
> upon the consciousness of the man for whom *things* have
> most meaning, for time is the fourth dimension of things. It
> may well be that [people] in primitive cultures which possess
> less of the material wealth, but compensate for this by hav-
> ing a greater social consciousness (a kind of a wealth of the
> spirit), are for this very reason less aware of the passage of
> time.[22]

The validity of the choleric vision of the future lies in the goal
toward which it propels us. Only that can justify the sacrifice of
the past and the present in the rush to get there. Since the
seventeenth century there has been a general agreement on
what that goal is. Both the progressive, future-oriented element in Western society and those dedicated to the Christian
goal of history hoped to see man living in freedom, harmony
and plenty. Modern science, commerce and theology all com-
bined to make that goal appear not only good and desirable,
but also possible.

It is time to ask ourselves, however, what many non-Western
Christians such as Mbiti and Koyama have been trying to
point out to us. Have we mistaken the American Dream for the
kingdom of God?

4. The Choleric Culture

Progress is still a very young "deity," born in an age of great material achievement and swaddled in the hypothesis of social evolution.
EUGENE A. NIDA, CUSTOMS AND CULTURES

It takes application, a fine sense of value, and a powerful community spirit for a people to have a serious leisure, and this has not been the genius of the Americans.
PAUL GOODMAN, GROWING UP ABSURD

Religion brought forth prosperity; and then the daughter destroyed the mother.
COTTON MATHER, MAGNALIA CHRISTI AMERICANA *(1702)*

Would you offer an excuse for arriving fifteen minutes late for a business appointment? You probably would, and a good one too. To be *that* late is a social offense, a form of insult. But would you bother to give an excuse if you arrived only five minutes late? Probably not. Five minutes is not considered a socially significant period of time. It involves no insult to a person's status or worth.

As little as twenty years ago, fifteen minutes was considered a basic time unit in urban America. A person showing up only ten minutes late for an appointment would not be considered late and would not even mumble an apology. But now, especially in urban areas of the United States, socially significant units of time are smaller, and a person arriving ten minutes after the appointed hour will offer some explanation.

Our whole society is moving toward a greater compression of time units. We can hardly imagine life in the time when clocks had only an hour hand. Ask what time it is and seldom will someone say, "It's about six thirty." Today if you ask someone the time, he will glance at his watch and say, "six thirty-three," and if he is especially mischievous, he will continue "and twenty-four seconds." Whereas a century ago an entire village was kept aware of the time by the pealing of the church bell, now each individual is alerted to the hour by a high-pitched beeper on his wrist watch. And since no two watches are set exactly alike, they announce each hour of board meetings and dinner parties with the erratic peeps of newly hatched chickens.

This mania for precision and punctuality began at the time of the industrial revolution when the need to synchronize different but related activities became paramount. The change from a rural to an industrial society drew people away from the cyclical rhythm of the soil and the seasons, imposing industry's own rhythm of linear, regular and measurable units of time. Improvements in the calendar and clocks, and the need to coordinate the work of masses of people and machines, brought about a complete reorientation in industrial societies, which still continues.

Consider: do women have an inherently different conception of time than men? Husbands who have spent time waiting for their wives to get ready might think so, and the number of jokes which have surrounded this phenomenon for centuries make it appear to be a universal characteristic. Samuel Pepys has this entry in his diary in the 1660s:

> Up, and my wife, a little before 4, and to make us ready; and
> by and by Mrs. Turner come to us, by appointment, and
> she and I staid talking below, while my wife dressed herself,

which vexed me that she was so long about it, keeping us till past 5 o'clock before she was ready.[1]

Sociologist-futurologist Alvin Toffler offers an explanation for the seemingly relaxed view that many women have toward the passing of chronological time and imposed deadlines. He suggests that because men had to make a more radical adjustment to industrial society, they had to become accustomed to the rigors of the clock more completely and more quickly than did women. Women were expected to care for children, who are notoriously unconscious of the demands of time, and to perform other household duties not controlled by the rigidity of the clock. Because of this, women were able to keep touch with the natural rhythms of life longer than men, who were largely deprived of them.[2]

It is the role of the person—career worker or homemaker —rather than gender that makes the difference in time orientation. The modern businesswoman is not amused by references to tardiness as innately characteristic of her sex. She has the same time demands as her male companions and office workers and has proved to be as responsibly time conscious as the male members of the work force.

Capitalistic Time

G. T. Whitrow, in his excellent study on Einstein's theories relating to time, gives ample attention to the change in the perception of time which occurred because of scientific and social changes. He contends that "the linear concept [of time] was fostered by the mercantile class and the rise of money economy."[3] As trade and commerce grew, the idea of wealth was dissociated from the land; and the faster that goods and services revolved, the faster one's wealth could grow, creating time pressure, what Lawrence Wright calls "the chains of chronarchy." So mobility and commerce increased the tempo of life, and Western man regarded time as valuable—and as constantly slipping away.

Scientific developments, too, contributed to the decline of

the cyclical, event-oriented view of time. Reliance on the mechanical clock, for example, increasingly dissociated the passage of time from human or natural events and helped us feel that time was external, objective and linear.

Commerce called to science for help when it faced critical mechanical problems. The English Board of Longitude in 1714 promised the award of 20,000 pounds to anyone who could develop a timepiece that would remain accurate within half a degree on a trip between the British Isles and the West Indies. The prize was finally awarded to John Harrison in 1773. It was but one of many financial encouragements the industrial society offered to technological development.

Yet acceptance of the new pace of life was neither uniform nor universal. There were riots in industrial cities and "machine bustings" by angry workers. Sensitive observers such as John Woolman, the American Quaker, lamented abuses justified by haste and punctuality:

> Stage-coaches frequently go upwards of one hundred miles in 24 hours and I have heard Friends say in several places that it is common for horses to be killed with hard driving. ... So great is the hurry in the spirit of.this world that in aiming to do business quickly and to gain wealth the Creation at this day doth loudly groan.[4]

In many places, the traditional event-oriented patterns continued outside the factory, and language often preserved the old values even where they had largely disappeared in practice. For example, in nineteenth-century England people still spoke of "a paternoster while"—the time necessary for a prayer. This is as event-oriented an expression as "a rice cooking" is in Madagascar today.[5] Today we know the length of a second by our sweep-second hands or pulsating digital watches. But we may still use colorfully imprecise expressions like "the shake of a mare's tail," or "as fast as you can say 'Jack Robinson.'"

We must conclude that the view of time which the future-oriented Westerner regards as obvious and natural is really neither ancient nor universally accepted. On the contrary, our linear, advancing view of time emerged in a small corner of the world just a few centuries ago. Although it certainly has had great acceptance and has unquestionably allowed valuable advances in science and technology, it is not a view shared by the majority of humanity. Nor should it be taken for granted as the best way to measure what is really important in our lives. It reflects the values of the choleric personality type, values which have come to dominate the thinking of an entire culture and have imposed its rhythm on an ever increasing number of people worldwide.

The Churches and Time Management

Theology also contributed to the view that time is a limited resource. Although Aristotle's view of time had dominated the philosophy of the Middle Ages, by the time of the Reformation Christian thinkers were not satisfied to consider time in just an abstract philosophical sense. In the Reformers' view, people as stewards before God were to employ and account for their time. Luther emphasized the value of work, and, according to sociologist Robert K. Merton, Calvin's emphasis on the stewardship of time stimulated the development of the watch industry in Geneva.[6] Theology entered the marketplace, and time became utilitarian.

The Protestant ethic as a whole, so influential in the development of capitalism, emerged in a society that *preceded* the modern industrial order. Capitalism did not create the virtues of responsibility, hard work and respect, but it relied on them and absorbed them. They were in keeping with the emerging industrial vision of man and progress—the progress which included the expansion of the kingdom of God with the implantation of Christian culture around the world.[7]

For Western people, the control of time is part of the original biblical mandate: time is to be dominated, subdued and ruled over like the rest of nature (Gen 1:28). Time is a resource at our disposal, to be used and exploited under careful management. Sound administration of resources is a given in a future-oriented, choleric culture; and time is to be considered as precious a resource as money, people or petroleum. Humanity has the responsibility to "redeem the time" (Eph 5:16; Col 4:5), and that means to do more with it.

The churches, while contributing to this understanding of time, were slow to put it into practice themselves. Centuries of tradition and prescribed rituals took precedence over planning the future of the church. Eternity, not time, preoccupied the seminaries, mission agencies and churches. After all, God's realm is spiritual and not to be administered as if it were a business concern. Christians, of course, were to "redeem the time," but that meant doing more religious things with it.

A quick look around churches today, however, shows how they have caught up with the secular world in their regard for time management. What Christian worker feels complete without his Success Diary or planning calendar? No longer can the preacher turn the hourglass over in order to keep on preaching for another hour; today's worship services are chronometerized beforehand so that they will exactly fit the space of sixty minutes. Prayer is a scheduled activity. Many churches use computers to provide efficiency. Many priests and ministers suffer from burnout, succumbing to the same temptations of "time macho" as their secular counterparts.[8]

Many of the modern apostles of Christian time management began their careers in business. Edward R. Dayton, co-author of *The Art of Management for Christian Leaders,* was in secular management for over a decade before doing theological studies. John C. DeBoer began a career in management in the aerospace industry before he studied theology. He has drawn parallels between biblical stewardship and sound administrative principles in his book with the intriguing title *How to Succeed in the Organization Jungle without Losing Your Religion.*

These men have been raised on Peter Drucker and other managers who accept the importance of moral values in the administration of a business.[9] By similar thinking, they insist that sound management principles can be applied to a spiritual enterprise. It is not a question of values, but only of good stewardship. Edward Dayton argues:

> I don't think there is a Christian philosophy of management any more than I think there is a Christian philosophy of bus driving. . . . Now, there no doubt are men in management (both secular and Christian) who are operating in very unchristian ways. . . . But as I read most current management theory, it seems very Christian indeed! . . . The failure is not in the philosophy, or lack thereof, but in the practice.[10]

These men were aghast to discover vast numbers of poorly administered churches, schools and mission societies. They were certainly less than impressed with those who justified religious unorganization because of its being a spiritual enterprise. So, for more than thirty years now, these Christian managers have been drawing on the wisdom of their secular but principled colleagues to awaken the Christian public in general, and organizational leaders in particular, to the blessings of getting things done decently, in order and efficiently.

Putting Time Tools to Work

In spite of reactionary cries of "you are bringing the world into the church," the wave of evangelical business expertise has taken the day. Now seminars on time management conducted by evangelicals equal any offered in the business world. Ted Engstrom and Alec Mackenzie's book *Managing Your Time* has sold thousands of copies and has been translated into numerous languages. PERT (Program Evaluation and Review Technique) charts are used worldwide for everything from organizing a picnic to preparing for a citywide evangelistic crusade. For those who want their timely tips in bite-size portions, there are the *Christian Leadership Newsletter* and seminars on cassette (so that you can save time by listening to them in your car). Christians have applied managerial principles to housekeeping, with books for homemakers which sound like Heloise's hints with a quiet time added. Evangelicals who made their peace with Madison Avenue some time ago are now equally comfortable on Wall Street.

Time management and goal setting have proved useful not only in eliminating sloppy organization in Christian enterprises, but also in redirecting the church's attention toward the future. Traditional ways of doing things are being questioned, and we want now to have unity in organizational as well as creedal terms. There is renewed interest in the "end of time," which at once relativizes all our plans and also focuses our future activities. Because of this, even such a cogent critic of technological society as Jacques Ellul can see the place for management tools. "Our technical discoveries are never anything more than temporary expedients which need to be put in their right place in the perspective of the Kingdom. But 'to put them in their right place' implies that there are secondary aims limited to these instruments. They are of *some* use."[11]

Therefore, we must not be hasty to dismiss the gift of administration (Rom 12:8) as a lesser gift or to curl our lip in disdain when we hear words like "organized" or "businesslike" used of Christian groups. If the tools are used for their intended purpose, they need not hinder the church's task, but should in fact help free it to do its job better.

Karen Mains, in her delightful book *Open Heart, Open Home,* illustrates how biblical principles and personal management have gone well together. She keeps a true biblical perspective, distinguishing between "hospitality" (Rom 12:13) with its concern for service and "entertaining" with its inherent interest in impressing others. She also affirms the importance of using time-management tools. While she wanted to avoid the pressure of trying to get everything "just right," a pressure which goes with entertaining, she still needed to get herself organized if she was going to exercise her gift of hospitality. The clincher was this: if she wanted to expand her ministry by writing a book to help others serve, she had to drastically reduce her hospitality! "I find that I cannot write about hospitality and be hospitable at the same time."[12]

Priorities, goals, planning—the tools of time management

—are powerful forces for the church's future if they are subjected to the goals of the kingdom of God.

Nevertheless we still wonder: are the goals of the kingdom still in sight? Are our failures in time stewardship really in the area of practice, as Dayton suggests, or can we question whether the theory is as benign as he proposes? Did Karen Mains expand her ministry, or did she sacrifice it? Could it be that the church's view of the future does not come from the biblical concept of "thy kingdom come," but rather from a triumphalistic cultural bias dominated by a future-oriented world view?

Many Christian writers have, unfortunately, accepted these tools uncritically. Notice how many recent books on management by evangelicals incorporate the humanist ideals of Alan Lakein's *How to Get Control of Your Time and Your Life*. What good is it for people to control their time and their lives, yet forfeit their souls? Even Edward Dayton now warns that many writers "have picked up the management tools of the world and dropped them into the church setting without passing them through a 'biblical filter.' "[13] There may indeed be need for more than blind acceptance of even the best of the time-management tools.

Objections to Future-Orientation

There are three major reasons why I question the future-oriented, managerial view of time, especially as applied to Christian management. The first is that this view regards time as a mere resource, similar to the earth's limited natural resources. Second, the triumphalism of the future-oriented society makes me wary of its vision of the future. Third, time managers are overly concerned with perfecting the means, having uncritically accepted the ends inherent in this shiny vision of the future.

Time as a resource.   To consider time a mere resource, like natural gas or chromium, is to see it as limited and subject to "running out." If we want to use it better, we must speed up the rhythm of life, since it comes to us only in measured quantities. "Redeeming" time comes to mean "gaining" time, that is, squeezing more out of it; and life becomes compressed and breathless. Time is also precious, to be spent with care, controlled. Yet it seems that as the rhythm of life increases (to save time), we must spend our allotment of time more quickly so that what we are trying to preserve becomes more scarce and more pressured—just the opposite of what we want. Just what supply of time have you stored up with your latest time-saving device? When we try to squeeze more out of time, the "more" we squeeze may be life itself.

> There is no living when you're nagging time
> And stunting every second with your will.[14]

To think of time as a gift instead of a resource does not mean that we would treasure it less or be careless with it. Rather, we would try to respect the wishes of the Giver by the way we use it. The resource view of time does maintain the idea of accountability, but it is a ledger-book accountability. It has lost the element of relationship, of stewardship in the personal sense as opposed to a hierarchical sense. A consequence of this is that we have confused the biblical idea of timing *(kairos)* with scheduling, and the biblical idea of rest with leisure.

Timing refers to the arranging of things in order, or the coming together of events in a fortuitous way. It is the "right time" or "appropriate season" so common in the Bible. Scheduling is also a way of putting things in order, but it does so by keeping them separate, not bringing them together. "By scheduling, we compartmentalize; this makes it possible to concentrate on one thing at a time, but it also deprives us of context."[15] When we equate the schedule, the linear order of events, with life itself, our view of reality shrinks and thought itself becomes divided into segmented compartments. The difference between biblical timing and secular scheduling is the difference between our ideas "in the wild" and in our own zoo. Caged ideas are much easier to study and organize, but they lose their vigor and excitement.

The Bible says almost nothing about leisure, but it has a great deal to say about rest. In the same way that God both works and rests at one and the same time (compare Gen 2:2 with Jn 5:17), so also we are to experience God's rest, at least in part, in the midst of our work (Heb 4:9-11). There *is* a scheduled rest, the seventh day, as a sign both of God's nature and of the complete rest which is ours to enjoy with our Creator. But it is not an arbitrary time period. It is a recurring "right time" established by God for our good.

When people begin to schedule their own leisure, that regular time for rest seems to disappear. It gets consumed in frenzied "leisure activities." Our society is hurrying faster and faster in order to create more leisure in which people then exhaust themselves. The alternative is to rediscover the biblical understanding of rest.

The choleric view of the future. My second objection to the future-oriented idea of time and its projections is that choleric (future-oriented) personalities are overconfident in the shape of the future toward which they lead us. Peter Drucker explains the logic of our futurist society: "To try to make the future happen is risky; but it is a rational activity. And it is less risky than coasting along on the comfortable assumption that nothing is going to change."[16]

That change will come is certain, but should we label it progress? The very association of the two in the minds of the future-oriented personality is a matter of concern:

> Because the future is their natural home, [choleric types] are more likely, when intelligent, psychologically stable and truly ethical, to be right about the future than are equally gifted members of other types. But they can also be unbelievably wrong, and lead an entire group toward a future which contains horror, despair and death.[17]

We have no desire to bring to mind such choleric-inspired tragedies as Jonestown or Hitler's Germany. Undoubtedly, examples of the positive side of this character type could be given, too. But that is not the point. The point is that these historical occurrences, and the future toward which we now are moving, were planned long before by those who are concerned to make the future happen. What we will pass through in the next few years will be but the consequences of decisions being made now, or already made, in quiet surroundings, by people calmly contemplating what they want to come to pass. Lawrence Wright sounds a warning note in his *Clockwork Man:*

> The doctrine of Progress...survives chiefly in the USA and the USSR, where rapid expansion and material prosperity have led (as they did in Victorian England) to a smug assumption of a mission to lead the world, to drive it by force if need be, towards a rosy future.[18]

Can we feel secure with the decisions now being made in Washington, Moscow and other power centers of the world? Toffler sees two common conclusions about the future: (1) "more of the same," the increased expansion of the industrial revolution over the globe, and (2) self-destruction, the earth "racing toward its final cataclysmic shudder."[19] Both options appear diabolically unattractive.

C. S. Lewis shared his concern for the direction toward which today's decision makers are leading us in an introduction which appears in only a few editions of his classic on infernal administration, *The Screwtape Letters.* Explaining why he used the image of a "thoroughly nasty business concern" to describe hell's organization he says:

> I live in the Managerial Age, in a world of "Admin." The greatest evil is not now done in those sordid "dens of crime" that Dickens loved to paint. It is not done even in concentration camps and labour camps. In those we see its final result. But it is conceived and ordered (moved, seconded, carried, and minuted) by quiet men with white collars and cut fingernails and smooth-shaven cheeks who do not need to raise their voices.[20]

We would like to think that Armageddon is being conceived in some hellish Babylon. But could the committee meetings and board rooms of America's churches and denominations be contributing toward such a grim future? J. Stanley Glen's *Justification by Success* supports the idea that they could. In this book Glen argues powerfully that the church has been secretly married to the power structures of the world:

> The captivity of the New Middle Class implicit in the suburban captivity of the churches is indirectly and subliminally a captivity of the church in general by companies and corporations. . . . It shapes the political and social outlook, the consciousness and thought of church-going people of this type. It influences their Christian life, work and worship deeply and subliminally. The reality of the captivity lies beneath the surface. It is never mentioned in the message, teaching, policy or practice of the church. But let any courageous preacher reveal what Jesus and certain of the apostles and prophets taught concerning the rich and the poor, the oppression of the latter by the former, about the love of money and how hard it is for the rich to enter the kingdom of God, and the reaction would probably be quick and severe.[21]

The means and the end.   Even when the church is blessed with "intelligent, psychologically stable and truly ethical" futurologists, we may still wonder if they are not concerned with a very short-range future. After all, they can only plan for as far as they can see, and even then, of course, the future is notoriously uncertain.

Time-management books, including Christian ones, either assume you already know what the main goals of life are, or else they leave it for you to decide them for yourself. Although not a Christian, Alan Lakein illustrates the approach:

> I'm not necessarily trying to show you how to become president of your company or how to juggle simultaneous careers as office worker and mother. With my system, you *can* achieve such goals—if they really are your goals. But you can also become a more effective college student, chess player, candle-maker or international playboy. It's entirely up to you.[22]

For the short haul, Lakein and the evangelical time managers
are quite right. Their techniques work. You can get an amazing amount done, eliminate time wasters and "find time" for a
host of things you have wanted to do. Christians and non-
Christians alike testify to the value of goal setting, determin-
ing priorities and planning as a way of bringing order out of
the chaos of their lives. As Ellul allowed, these tools "are of
some use." We might even want to say "*a lot of* use."

Sooner or later, however, if we are even a bit reflective, we
may wonder if we are heading toward the right objective. Are
our goals really what are significant in life? It is an agonizing
moment; we may discover that the short-range goals we have
set for ourselves are not really our own, but are just a reflection
of society's rootless values, or else that all we have done is
dedicated to our own egos. Our goals may prove to be nothing
more than a "game plan" drawn up without really knowing the
object of the game.

No matter how pleased we may be with our improvements
as we "get our act together," these plans work only to the extent that they become a law which governs all our decisions
and actions. By obeying these self-imposed laws, we reach the
goal, and we feel justified. But like the law in the Old Testament, it is good—but it brings death, not life. This is so for two
reasons:

1. To the extent that our goals are for self-development, we
are trying to do for ourselves what God wants to do in us. Earl
Jaboy in *The Kingdom of Self* laments that

> there are multitudes of religious people in the world who
> right this moment are knocking themselves out with their
> good deeds, their philanthropies and their religious rituals.
> Good as these self-chosen acts are, if they are not preceded
> by the act of surrender of the will to God's rule, the doer is
> working himself into a terrible delusion.[23]

If, of course, we *have* surrendered to the will of God's rule,
then we will be "fulfilling the only mission with which [we]
have been charged by Jesus Christ, which is first of all *to be a*

sign,"[24] which has nothing to do with self-development. The goal can never be the "kingdom of self"; only the kingdom of God will answer.

2. If our goals are in the area of action, of achievement, service and leadership, we are bound to fail. It is not a matter of having set our personal goals too high, because we can always reduce them to scale; or, since they are our own goals, we can forgive ourselves for not reaching them. No, the sense of anxiety or guilt we sometimes feel when we evaluate our past performance comes from the doubt that maybe we haven't chosen the right goals at all.

The solution is not to give up having any goals at all, nor is it to punish ourselves for failure. The answer is grace, which we need on two levels: first in the sense of a "grace period" in our contracts, programs and schedules. This is a way of affirming that people are more important than the programs we devise ostensibly to serve them. Second, and more comprehensive, we need grace in its theological sense, the experience of God's forgiveness for having failed to reach *his* goals. For that, we need to know what his goals are, which is the purpose of the next section.

Part II.
Time and Signs of the Kingdom

5. The Kingdom of Opportunity

Unless hope has been roused and is alive there can be no stimulation for planning.
JUERGEN MOLTMANN, HOPE AND PLANNING

*Alice sighed wearily. "I think you might do something better with time," she said,
"than wasting it asking riddles with no answers." "If you knew Time
as well as I do," said the Hatter, "you wouldn't talk about wasting it. It's him."*
LEWIS CARROLL, ALICE'S ADVENTURES IN WONDERLAND

Time never takes time off.
AUGUSTINE OF HIPPO

The minor Greek god *kairos* was represented by the statue
of a young man with wings on his feet and a tuft of hair on the
top of his forehead. The word *kairos* means "time," or "opportunity," and these sculptured features give us some idea of how
the Greeks viewed the passing of time. The wings indicated
that opportunity passes swiftly. Time, as the opportune or
fitting moment, is fleeting. The exaggerated forelock implied
the need for decision, for seizing the occasion. Before the moment passes by, we must grab it by the hair. It is this picture of

the Greek idea of time which prompted Fedro to comment, "Opportunity may have hair in front, but he is bald in back."

How do we picture the God of the Bible? We don't. God is not static, nor is he limited by his creation, and so there can be no adequate spatial representation of him. Rather, God reveals himself in history. He has acted and continues to be active. He has chosen to represent himself to us as a verb rather than a noun, and as a verb of being (relation) rather than of doing (sequence), as his name suggests: "I am who I am" or, as many commentators suggest, "I will be what I will be" (Ex 3:14). It is no accident that when God created the world he did not designate a holy *place,* but rather a holy *time*—the seventh day (Gen 2:2-3).[1]

The Greeks, like the Hebrews, determined the passage of time by the movement of the sun and the moon. They referred to these as heavenly *bodies,* as just more bits of matter in the universe; their whole view of time was quite philosophical, with a streak of pessimism. The Greek verb tenses allow for exact divisions of past, present and future, which should have given a good base for a sophisticated sense of history. Yet there was a tendency to see time as circular or to visualize it spatially, and no clear sense of history developed.[2] Perhaps we can think of the Greeks as somewhat phlegmatic, reflecting on the passage of time without much feeling or commitment to it.

The Hebrews, on the other hand, referred to the sun and moon as *lights* (Gen 1:14-19; Ps 136:7-9), which are signs of God's goodness as well as his glory and power. The passing of time to the Hebrews was not a threat or source of anxiety; it contained elements of hope because God was acting in history:

"For I know the plans I have for you," declares the LORD, "plans to prosper you and not to harm you, plans to give you hope and a future." (Jer 29:11)

Know also that wisdom is sweet to your soul;/if you find it, there is a future hope for you,/and your hope will not be cut off. (Prov 24:14)

In these two passages, the chronology of the future is not so important as the content of the future, which is seen as a gift or reward from God. Throughout the Old Testament it is not an abstract idea of time which has meaning, but instead it is "the use made of the historical sequence for the presentation of an encounter with God."[3] The verb structure of the Hebrew language is very different from that of the Greek. Hebrew is not so concerned with past, present and future; instead it distinguishes between events completed and those not yet completed, reflecting an event-oriented culture. Often, what we would call the past tense, that is, the tense to describe a completed event, is used for the future when God is declaring what is yet to happen. This "prophetic perfect" indicates that God's promises are so sure that they can be said to have happened already.

God's promises, to be fulfilled "later," gave a sense of expectancy to time. It meant that some events had more weight or significance than others. Not that chronological time was unimportant, but that the passing time had a certain quality about it, and some moments were more expressive than others because the promise implied a goal.

And having a goal meant that the significance of time increased, or matured, with the passing of chronological time. Time was pregnant with eternity. God was going to keep his promise.

Chronos and Kairos

The New Testament uses the two most common Greek words for time, *chronos* and *kairos,* to distinguish between two aspects: (1) the chronological, everyday events, what we undisparagingly call clock time, and (2) the special occurrences, or seasons, in the life of a person or of the nation. *Chronos* referred to the linear expanse, a period or space of time, and was used for "formal and scientific conception of time."[4] *Kairos,* on the other hand, indicated more the idea of right time, or opportunity, such as "the time for figs" (Mk 11:13).

Early studies on the biblical view of time tried to make a

clear distinction between these words based on their etymology in order to show that for the Bible *chronos,* or the formal passing of time, was not really important. They tried to show that *kairos,* with its inherent idea of "right time" or opportunity, is what really gave significance to their lives. But James Barr has done us all a favor by showing from actual biblical usage that the word *kairos* is a polysemy, that is, a word with more than one meaning.[5] It *can* mean the decisive or right time, but more commonly it refers to time in general, a synonym for *chronos.*[6]

The word for "hour" *(hōra),* with which we are more familiar, can illustrate this. *Hōra* can refer to a specific, measurable length of time, or it can figuratively mean a short time or moment ("at that very hour"). Both of these are close to the idea of *chronos.* Yet *hōra* can also have a more *kairos*-type of meaning: "It is the hour"; that is, "it is high time." The context makes all the difference.

We can conclude that there is no legitimate distinction between the Greek and Hebrew conception of time on the basis of these two words alone. After all, they are both Greek words! While the quality of time, or the importance of a specific occasion, may be more important than just a string of passing moments, it is chronology, the order of history, that gives the context for decisive events.

Nevertheless, the word *kairos* takes on a special meaning in some places in the New Testament because of its application to the fulfillment of God's promises, and so it merits more careful attention. The origin of the word includes the meanings of right measure and correct proportion, that which is convenient, appropriate or fitting. It could be used in positive contexts to signal opportunity or an advantageous situation, or in negative contexts to mean danger.

It appears that people from event-oriented cultures grasp more completely the depth of meaning in this word. The Chinese word *weiji,* for example, means "dangerous opportunity."[7] The Japanese theologian Kosuke Koyama uses the same idea to describe the importance of Jesus' temptation in the wilderness and stresses the importance of this concept for presenting Christianity in the Orient.[8] In English, the word *timing* (as opposed to just *time*) has been suggested, and in some contexts it works.[9] In most places, however, the word *opportunity* comes closest. In secular usage it would have the idea of "fortuitous," timely; for the Christian, however, there is nothing "chancey" about it. God's activity is behind it.

In the Old Testament, Esther 4:14 provides a case in point. To those outside the Jewish community, Esther's presence in the palace right when the Jewish people were threatened would be just luck or chance, but it was not so for God's people. "Who knows but that you have come to royal position for such a time as this?" Here the idea is of a "divine initiative for creating an opportune situation within the course of the individual's life."[10]

In the New Testament we see that Jesus has this sense of time "being ripe." His brothers urged him to attend the Feast of Tabernacles, but Jesus replied, "The right time for me has not yet come; for you any time is right. . . . You go to the Feast. I am not yet going up to this Feast, because for me the right time has not yet come" (Jn 7:6, 8). The idea of *kairos* (although not the word itself) may be behind many of his parables, such as those of the thief in the night (Mt 24:42-44), the ten virgins (Mt 25:1-13) and the talents (Mt 25:14-30).

Kairos is a word heavy with hope. Therefore it is not surprising that as Jesus began his public ministry, this word would be used to explain the meaning of his hour in history: "The time has come. The kingdom of God is near" (Mk 1:15).

The Timing of the Kingdom
The message of the kingdom of God struck a responsive chord of expectation in his hearers. The idea that time had matured, that it was being fulfilled at that moment, called for a response, a decision to appropriate what had long been awaited. Jesus suggested the appropriate response: "Repent and believe the

good news!" (Mk 1:15; cf. Mt 4:17).

The Hebrews had long recognized God's sovereign rule over his creation and over all of human history. The idea of his universal kingship permeates the Old Testament (Josh 2:11; Ps 103:19; 145:11-13; Is 37:16; Dan 6:26). Yet they longed for "that day" when his glory would be revealed to all men (Is 24:21-23) and his lordship would be universally recognized (Zech 14:9). They had every expectation of being the saints who would share in the eternal kingdom as promised in Daniel (2:44; 7:27).

There was a dark, foreboding aspect to the "day of God's visitation" because it would be a time when he would exercise judgment (Is 10:3; 13:9; Ezek 7:19). Jesus did not contradict those dark prophecies (Mt 7:21-23; 10:15; Mk 13:24-26), but he did announce resurrection on the basis of his authority as the Son of Man, which introduced a new element of hope (Jn 5:27; 6:39-40, 44-54; 11:24; Mt 16:27-28). Repentance is a form of death and judgment in the present which will transform the fearsome "day of the Lord" into the joyful, victorious "day of the Lord Jesus" (2 Cor 1:14; Phil 1:4-6).

It is important not to separate God's *kairos* from the presence of the kingdom. In Mark 1:15 the Greek connects the two phrases: "The time is fulfilled, and the kingdom of God is at hand" (RSV). This means, first, that the kingdom of God is not some spiritual, that is, atemporal, realm far from human concerns. Second, the kingdom is not here on earth just anywhere or anytime. In Jesus of Nazareth the time of the kingdom arrived. Jesus' authoritative teaching, his power over the forces of Satan and his other miracles were signs that the kingdom had come (Mt 11:4-5; 12:28; Mk 1:27). Because of his presence he could announce "the kingdom of God is in your midst" (Lk 17:21 NASB), and so the blessings of the kingdom—salvation, forgiveness and eternal life—were immediately available.

Did the kingdom end with Jesus' death? Or did Jesus change his message, postponing the coming of the kingdom because of the unbelief of his hearers? By no means. The Lord's Prayer equates the kingdom with doing the will of God, such that the kingdom is revealed wherever there is submission to God as King. The kingdom continued to be an important theme in the teaching of the early church (Acts 8:12; 20:25; 28:23, 31; Col 1:13; 1 Thess 2:12; James 2:5).

Although the phrase becomes rare in the epistles and refers most frequently to the final manifestation of the kingdom in all its power and glory, the teaching of our present submission to Christ's lordship and obedience to the gospel by the regenerating power of the Holy Spirit is a prominent theme. Hebrews uses Old Testament images to show that we enjoy today the first fruits of the heavenly state (Heb 3:3-6; 10:11-14; 12:22-24). Other apostolic writers use other images, but they all elaborate aspects of the kingdom as Jesus preached it (2 Cor 5:17-21; 1 Pet 2:9-10; 1 Jn 3:1-2).

Yet, for all the "good news" which the present expression of the kingdom is, it is still only a glimpse of the final perfection which Christ will bring about on the final day. Jesus made it clear that the full realization of the kingdom is future (Mt 6:10), that men are to seek it, even strive for it (Mt 6:33; Lk 13:24), and that sacrifice is worthwhile in order to gain it (Mt 13:44-46; Mk 9:47). But men by their own efforts will never build the kingdom. It is a gift from God, to be completed in his time (Mt 25:34; Mk 10:15; Lk 12:32; 19:11). It is on the basis of this expectation of the future kingdom that there is so much speculation concerning the "last days."

The Significance of the Kingdom for Time
The kingdom of God is the biblical image of God's rule most closely linked with the time of fulfillment *(kairos)*. The Old Testament writers, Jesus and the apostles all announced its present reality and imminent completion.

What does all this have to do with our goals, our temperaments or the planning and use of our time? Just this: The kingdom fulfills the highest hopes of humanity for an "age of righteousness and peace" in which time becomes a friend and no longer an enemy. God has already begun to establish his kingdom, and all we do should be related to it. As Andrew Kirk has expressed it, "Christian theology is seeking to ascertain which elements of the Biblical message speak most directly to aspirations for social justice, revolutionary change and a utopian future. The kingdom tops the list of candidates."[11]

The goals of the kingdom are so attractive it is no surprise that manmade counterfeits have emerged. Marxism appeals to the same aspiration. It announces its own "decisive moment" *(kairos)* in the present because it is "possessed by a messianic sense," says Samuel Escobar. "It sees the particular historical moment in which it appears as a moment filled with revelatory and decisive meaning. Second, the uniqueness of this moment is related to the end of history that gives meaning to the process of which it is a part. Third, part of the uniqueness of this moment is that at this point the necessary tools have been developed for an enlightened view of reality that surpasses all previous views."[12]

The appeal of Marxism is for the values of the kingdom—but without God. It is a counterfeit kingdom, but one closer to the biblical vision of the future than the capitalist dream. Christians must be careful to distinguish the false hopes of either ideology from the authentic signs of the kingdom of God.

As with any heresy, the solution lies in rediscovering the dynamic and scope of the biblical doctrine. The most fruitful response to the mutually contradictory determinism and self-effort implicit in the secular views of history is not to belabor the inconsistency, but rather to proclaim "Christ's claim that he makes all things new, and His call to us to be new people."[13] This newness begins within the life of a believer, but it must find expression in the world. Otherwise we cannot really be considered new people.

This leads us to consider the following consequences of our commitment to the coming of the kingdom, each of which I will deal with in succeeding chapters:

1. Time, like all other aspects of the creation, has experienced the effects of the Fall. "The days are evil" because they

have come under the control of the Evil One, and consequently our time must know the redeeming power of the Lord as much as our money, temperament or natural talents. Unfortunately, some Christian time managers have erroneously used Ephesians 5:16 and Colossians 4:5 as the biblical basis for their pleas that we use our time *(chronos)* better, not recognizing the scope of the word for time *(kairos)* which appears in those verses. "Redeeming the time" (KJV) is not referring primarily to the hours and minutes of the Christian's day, but rather to the opportunities which arise to extend the kingdom of God: "[Make] the most of every opportunity" (NIV).

Which opportunities are those? The context of the verses answers that question. By mistaking the sense of time in these verses (and of redemption, too, in regard to time), these undoubtedly good administrators have, perhaps unwittingly, led others to a cramping legalism in regard to time—to an efficient but frenzied, overscheduled existence and, worse, a life of unfulfilling activities. By understanding the *kairos* of these verses in the context of the kingdom we have new vistas to the dynamic life in the Spirit opened to us. Chapter six will look at these new vistas.

2. The kingdom of God gives us our goals, the unifying purpose which is so missing in Marxist or humanistic time-management plans. The kingdom calls us to humbly submit our plans to God's, to give up our resistance to his eternal purpose being worked out in history. The secular vision has no such accountability and doesn't want it. "Humanists . . . object particularly to the idea that we have reason to be ashamed before God, and that we need his forgiveness for our resistance to his loving claims on our priorities."[14] Time-management tools may well be effective means, once the ends are clear, but those ends do not come from the management skills themselves. Chapter seven will help us focus on our goal in Christ.

3. The Holy Spirit, who is the active agent of the kingdom in this age, provides the link of meaning or significance between the overall goal of God and the individual actions of the

millions of subjects in his kingdom. The Spirit interprets the Word to our present, so that the urgency which marked the Old Testament prophets and the urgency of the approach of the Final Day become the motivation to make right choices in the present. " 'That Day' past and future, has no other function than to illuminate 'today,' "[15] and the One who knows the future is the very One who aids us in our personal and corporate planning. We will look in chapter eight at some ways to plan our lives to better grasp kingdom opportunities.

6. Taking the Pressure off Redemption

It took me twice as long to write this book as I thought it would.
ALEC R. MACKENZIE, THE TIME TRAP

To be most effective, we must achieve maximum results in minimum time.
TED W. ENGSTROM, THE WORK TRAP

*If we had a "time-oriented" God, there would be a firm date
for the end of the world and God would keep it.*
MARVIN MAYERS

The word *kairos* appears in two verses commonly quoted by biblically minded time managers: Ephesians 5:16 and Colossians 4:5, both translated "Redeeming the time" in the King James Version. The New International Version and the New English Bible have been careful to bring out the general significance of *kairos* here, using the word *opportunity*. Weymouth keeps the root idea of redemption in his rendering, "Buy up your opportunities."

What we must realize is that there is no idea here of squeezing more activity into less time *(chronos)*. Unfortunately, J. B. Phillips's paraphrase (most quoted after the King James Version by evangelical writers on time management) has "Make the best possible use of your time," which, however wrongly understood, has encouraged those who want to interpret these verses to mean "Get more organized." Not that many of us would not profit from getting ourselves more organized; but we should not make these verses say "Do more, faster," as if clock time were the main focus. Such a time-conscious understanding would certainly be a modern imposition on the basically event-oriented biblical culture.

If we understand the word *kairos* as its better translation "opportunity," what is this opportunity which Paul urges the churches, and us, to redeem? First, in the context of Colossians 4:5 we see that it concerns our dealings with non-Christians, "outsiders." Paul is personally concerned about making the message of Christ clear wherever he is, and he wants the Colossians to do the same thing where they are. Paul urges the Colossians to be wise, to be "full of grace" in their conversation with unbelievers and to give fitting answers to their questions or accusations (Col 4:6). In this context they are to be discerning, perceptive of the opportunities, and to have appropriate, fitting explanations of their faith. It is a passage for apologists, not managers.

The context of Ephesians 5:16 also calls for wisdom, but here it does not refer so much to presenting Christ as to keeping alert against the inroads of evil from contact with the world. The Ephesians are to understand God's will, and that means having a right perspective on things, which is only possible if they are filled with the Spirit and not fuzzy headed with strong drink. There are decisions to be made, and we need clear heads for that. So here, as in Colossians, the emphasis is on discerning priorities. Certainly that has to do with our life management, as we keep clear our criteria of selection, but it is not a mandate to fit more uncritically accepted "good" activities into our lives.

We are, of course, to be active in the service of the King. But a cursory reading of the Sermon on the Mount or one of Paul's epistles leaves even the most energetic advocate of "victorious Christian living" with doubts about our ability to be faithful servants. It is like asking a missionary candidate to choose his field of service strictly on the basis of "need." He would have to be in a thousand places at once. Some limits and some decisions are necessary.

How to Be "Instant"
The same issue arises in regard to 2 Timothy 4:2, which in the King James Version reads, "Be instant in season, out of season." The word for "season" is again our word *kairos,* and so the sense is "whether the moment is opportune or not." A popular interpretation of this verse is that the Christian is to witness to unbelievers whether or not the situation is appropriate. Some evangelism seminars have taught that we are to barge in whether the target of our evangelism is interested or not; this has led to a lot of offensive tactics, unnecessary irritation on the part of unbelievers and guilt on the part of those Christians who could not bring themselves to be obnoxious for the sake of a word about the gentle Savior.

The context indicates that Paul was indeed urging Timothy not to be timid. He was to preach the gospel message boldly, to "press it home" (NEB). But the idea of *epistēthi* ("be prepared," NIV) is that of standing by, being ready, or being prepared or attentive because opportunity will be present just when you don't expect it. Again, as in the previous verses, there is the idea of preparedness, of being discerning, in order to take advantage of the fitting moment.

Yet when Paul considers the importance of preaching, he includes the unfitting moment ("out of season") as well. What does he mean here? The New English Bible captures well the sense when it says that Timothy is to be ready on all occasions "convenient or inconvenient." That is, convenient or inconvenient for *Timothy!* Opportunities will come "ready or not."

He must be prepared so that he can bring the word at the right time whether or not he finds it convenient.

Such an understanding of this verse does not reduce the urgency of the message nor the need to boldly seize opportunities that arise. All it does is to keep us from sanctifying rudeness and high-pressure tactics. People may still be offended by the message of the gospel, but they should not identify the message with the abrupt and artificial presentation of a pressured and pressuring evangelist who has no sense of what is appropriate.

For many, this pressure to witness whether or not anybody wants to listen comes from the example of those who are naturally outgoing and dynamic. Extroverts do not mean to impose their way on others, but they think of their ways as natural and so perhaps unconsciously communicate the ideal of an aggressive witnessing style. But people with different personalities should not be urged to deny their God-given gifts in order to conform to a "victorious witness" style which is unnatural for them. Rebecca Manley Pippert, in her best-selling guide to unpressured evangelism, has comfort for shy witnesses:

> Let God make you fully you. Rejoice in your God-given temperament and use it for God's purposes. God made some of us shy, others outgoing. We should praise him for that. But if you are shy, remember that your shyness is not an excuse to avoid relationships; rather it means you will love the world in a different way than an extrovert.[1]

The first reaction of some overburdened soul winner to this view of opportune moments and the importance of our temperament for sharing the gospel may be one of relief. And then, with the pressure off, he or she may feel no more compulsion to witness at all. Yet certainly that is not Paul's intention. Although the text does not support an artificial "instant replay" evangelism, it certainly does motivate us to an authentic witness which can happen at any time.

Invariably my best opportunities to witness to God's grace

come when I'm tired or busy. The moment may be timely from God's point of view, but it is inconvenient or embarrassing for me. Perhaps a tense situation needs a calm, biblical word, but I am either too excitedly involved or so fearfully withdrawn that I miss the opportunity and contribute nothing. But God calls me to be prepared and alert "ready or not" in any situation of human need or confusion. And that is far more challenging than forcing a situation and compelling myself to spout some canned formula to an unwilling audience.

Planning and Triumphalism

Perhaps the most disturbing aspect of this forced view of time redemption, whether applied to evangelism or any other area of the Christian life, is that it supports a triumphalistic view of the church's mission. We are told the following story: "The world may be going from bad to worse, but in the church the ministry is growing, people are being saved, programs are expanding and things are going to get better and better." It is another expression of the future-oriented dynamic of our society, enthusiastically steamrolling the church toward greater expansion, more effort and bigger plans. "Status symbol evangelism"—going after the youth idols—is just one example of this basically works-oriented approach: "Only the best is good enough for God." Mission budget dollar-soul equivalence is another.

Let there be no mistake: Christians praise God for conversions, growing churches and greater missionary efforts. Signs of God's ultimate victory *are* evident, and we rejoice in them. We are on the side of the God who triumphs. The problem with triumphalism, however, is that it does not give due recognition to the element of suffering in the fulfillment of the church's mission.

Both planning and hope are expressions of dissatisfaction with the present, but only hope sees redemptive purpose in suffering. Planning (or the lack of it) may cause suffering, but suffering really serves no purpose in the triumphalistic view of the future. It is merely unfortunate and to be avoided if possible. Biblical hope, however, includes the perception and acceptance of suffering as part of God's plan for his church and therefore for us personally (2 Cor 1:5-7; Col 1:24; 1 Pet 4:12-13). Planning can be biblical if it is accompanied by meekness and hope; the church "must recapture this view of God which places him above the times in all his majesty and power, and yet *in* the times in weakness and suffering hope."[2]

This means that the church must call a halt to its complicity with the world and its game called success-status-domination. The association of the church with the power structures of the world does not enhance its ministry but only discredits its ministry among those who so desperately need it. Christ's mission goes forward through the weak, the despised, the lowly; namely, through those who have adopted a servant attitude. Ellul uses Jesus' images of wolves and sheep to illustrate the difference:

> In the world everyone wants to be a "wolf" and no one is called to play the part of a "sheep." Yet the world cannot live without this living witness of sacrifice. That is why it is essential that Christians should be very careful not to be "wolves" in the spiritual sense—that is, people who try to dominate others.[3]

We need not try to invent some suffering in order to share in it. Suffering is already in ample supply. All we need to do is abandon the privileges of the "system," that is, of the domineering, future-grasping pseudogospel, and the world's suffering will become everywhere evident and compelling.

This is what "taking advantage of the opportunities" refers to in Ephesians 5:16 and Colossians 4:5. We must not stuff our schedule full of self-imposed duties. We are called to a life of constant alertness to the opportunities for bearing witness to the operation of the kingdom in this world. We need eyes to see them and a will trained to act. It is a matter of our inner time controlling the external time, and not vice versa.

Does this mean that the Christian assumes a life of misery

and chaos? Must he or she become available to others to the
point of exhaustion, or run around without any order or plan?
Of course not.

> As God has given ordered existence to nature, so he also
> gives man the occasion to lead an ordered life. But most men
> are rebellious and disorderly over against God and the situa-
> tions he offers them. Their life therefore seems futile. But
> the man who submits to God's will and accepts each occa-
> sion as a gift from God may lead a happy life in what the
> New Testament would call "faith."[4]

The self-imposed or, in most cases, tradition-imposed order of
our lives is what drives us and empties life of meaning (1 Pet
1:18). The life of faith has an order and an urgency all its own,
lived out in the same time frame as everyone else's; but by its
very nature this life, and the time it experiences, have the marks
of God's redemption.

Redeeming Lives and Time

The life of faith is possible only to those who have experienced
God's redeeming grace in Christ. Yet some areas of our lives
seem to respond more completely and quickly to the discipling
of the Spirit. Our time, like all of God's gifts so squandered by
the unregenerate man, must pass through the refining fires of
God's stern grace.

Redemption has the literal sense of "buying back," although
probably in the contexts of Ephesians 5:16 and Colossians 4:5
the marketplace connotation is not prominent. But the idea of
liberation is there. We are to buy up the opportunities, liberat-
ing time so that we can make good use of it, taking advantage
of the occasions which God brings.

Redemption is something which God is doing on a cosmic
scale (Heb 2:8-9) and which includes us as part of his plan (Heb
2:15; 2 Cor 5:17). We, along with the whole universe, are waiting for his final redemption (Rom 8:19-20). The idea of waiting implies that time *(chronos)* is also bound up in the effects
of the Fall: "the days are evil." Even though time as part of the

creation was good, it has been usurped by the Enemy, who now wants to control not only the passing of events in history, but also our own personal, inner time. Therefore we must "regain for fruitful use the days which the devil would misuse."[5]

If we must regain this time and make it our own again, it must have been lost; that is, it had come to mean nothing. Persons cut off from God are cut off from life, and though the clock keeps ticking and their hearts keep beating, there is no eternal significance to their activities. What does time mean to a dead person? "Without the mind and heart of man—brought to expression in the interpretive word—history is nothing but a chain of occurrences, aimless, void and futile."[6] What God is doing cosmically he is also doing in our own lives, and so we groan with the universe and wait patiently for the consummation of that which God has begun (Rom 8:18-25).

At the same time, redemption in Jesus Christ initiates a new life, one in which the life of God invades ours, making the passing of time take on the significance of eternity. We can see the design of history's tapestry even though the entire cloth is not yet woven, and we can be sure that the thread of our lives fits into his great design. Being saved is not so much a line to be crossed as a road to walk; it calls for faithful obedience to the promptings of the Spirit of life who knows both the "now" and the "yet to be." That is, we are called to redeem constantly that which was lost and dead in our lives, including our time. "Men are called to redeem the contents of life *in life,* to salvage life by working in time until the final time, to find meaning by making each hour of life a theo-temporal hour."[7]

It is not that we must pump time full of life again with our own activity. That is the way the world is doing it; and rather than find life in time, the world discovers that time becomes scarce, disappears and ends in remorse. We who are alive with God's life will also have God's time. Time itself will become alive again to us. That calls for a dramatically different view of life: a releasing of our inner time with a consequent sense of fulfillment in our tasks and the expectation of a complete "coming together" of all the redeemed time of the saints at the end.

    There is a reminder of the resurrection at the start
    of each new year, each new decade.
    That's why I also like sunrises, Mondays and new seasons.
    God seems to be saying,
    "With me you can always start afresh."[8]

In the present we can experience some of this fulfillment proclaimed by Christ "in the fullness of time": redemption, eternal life, hope. All this is but one aspect of the kingdom which he announced. There is another aspect, the future aspect, which determines the destination of history and provides us with the goals necessary to plan our individual lives.

7. Seeking First the Future of God

The greatest human need is not to learn how to get what we want, but rather to learn what we ought to want.
DONALD MACKAY, HUMAN SCIENCE AND HUMAN DIGNITY

God's calling does not tell us what to do. It drives us out from where we should not be.
CLAUDE TRESMONTANT, A STUDY OF HEBREW THOUGHT

The Stock Exchange is a poor substitute for the Holy Grail.
JOSEPH SCHUMPETER, THE CRISIS OF THE TAX STATE

The kingdom of God tells us where to focus our energies; it gives us our priorities. Both the present and the future aspects of the kingdom motivate us to live as joyous subjects in God's realm. The indwelling Spirit and the nearness of God's judgment are what determine our lifestyle. Paul sums up the first aspect in Romans 14:17: "The kingdom of God is not a matter of eating and drinking, but of righteousness, peace and joy in the Holy Spirit." And Peter expresses the urgency implicit in the latter, "Since everything will be destroyed in this way, what kind of people ought you to be? You ought to live holy and godly lives as you look forward to the day of God" (2 Pet 3:11-12a).

God's present rule in our lives is concerned primarily with the *quality* of our lives, in the sense of character. We are men and women "under reconstruction," and to the extent that we approach the image of Christ, our lifestyle will take on his un-hurried purposefulness. This is a lifelong process, but not in the sense of something happening "to" us. Rather, the priorities we choose to live by progressively shape and define who we are. Donald MacKay links the character of the kingdom with who we are becoming as we participate in it now and prepare for its future.

> What identifies me more fundamentally than anything else is my total "goal-complex" or priority-scheme: what defines and orders all my aims and satisfactions in life, great and small. . . . If when we leave this life there are priorities we cannot take with us, this will be no merely incidental loss; for it is these priorities that in part *define who we are.* . . . If we cherish, as an essential part of what identifies us, priorities which are incompatible with God's eternal kingdom, then when God says that someone with such priorities cannot enter his kingdom he is not being arbitrarily intolerant. He is saying simply that since such priorities can have no existence in the new kingdom, nobody to whom these priorities are essential can exist in it either. If we want to be realistic in obedience to the biblical perspective on human nature and human dignity, then, our chief concern will be that while there is time God's grace may cause to atrophy in us all priorities and desires unfit for eternity, replacing them with better ones, in order that we can survive the transplantation without loss of identify.[1]

Such control of our priorities would be difficult enough if it were strictly an individual matter. But it is a concern for the church as the body of Christ, as well. It is not just the individual Christian who can cease to be salt and light in the world.

An entire group of believers, organized to express corporately the presence of the kingdom in the present world, can lose its influence on the world and become indistinguishable from it (Rev 2:5). A church can be like "Cinderella with amnesia,"[2] called to be the bride of the coming King, but having forgotten the promises made her during the courtship. Thus it is essential that the churches remember their commission and determine their priorities accordingly.

The Church's Goals

Andrew Kirk has summarized the three main purposes of the church, and he fears that unless bold action is taken, these distinctives of God's people will be lost. The first he calls "the kingdom itself": the church exhibiting the values of the kingdom in the world as the visible expression of the character of God. It is a matter of faithfulness to the calling that the church be a separated people concerned with God's glory. "The free offer of forgiveness and new life is inseparable from the demand to reorient one's life completely around the values of the kingdom as manifested in the life of Jesus."[3]

Second, the church has the obligation to declare the good news throughout the entire world. God has given his people the task of world evangelization, and our efforts must concentrate on fulfilling that task with the utmost urgency. There are always many worthwhile things for the church to do, but they have always involved allocating resources to other than primary objectives. The church's leadership must ask first, What opportunities is God preparing for a favorable response to the gospel, and how can we best take advantage of them?

Third, the church has the responsibility to serve the poor and suffering. This is, perhaps, a logical consequence of the other two, since by representing God's concern for the world and by bearing the good news to all people, the church should automatically be caring for the poor and suffering. But in practice this logic has not always been consistently followed. Because we have neglected to serve the suffering in the past, Kirk emphasizes this third aspect separately.

To include this third item as a priority for the churches' agenda is not to create a tension between evangelism and social action. There is no either-or about it. The noted evangelist William Pannell has shown the dependence of one upon the other: "In order to preach Christ today the Church must be able to demonstrate a capacity to repent of her complicity with the world and its oppressive stratagems. The capacity for such repentance will determine the degree of her credibility to those held captive in injustice and violence."[4]

Pannell goes on to emphasize that such a concern for the oppressed is not a matter for just some people or some church agencies, or as a means to be relevant in modern society. It is a matter of the church's basic allegiance being worked out in the relationships and priorities of everyday life, because the church's call to selfless service is part of the original vocation of God's people. Linking Jesus' announcement of the kingdom to the prophecies of Luke 1, Pannell says, "Jesus' announcement of the 'time' and the incoming of the Kingdom of God was not an attempt to be 'relevant.' Rather, it was the divine initiative in time and in history to offer a radical alternative to the oppression of the times."[5]

This may sound as though it applies only to those responsible for administrating the resources of large churches or denominations. It does apply to them, of course, but it is equally valid for the individual believer. Every Christian should reserve time periodically for evaluation to review his priorities in light of the Scriptures and see whether the use of his or her time conforms to those priorities. Is all your time taken up in work, church committees, personal self-help programs, and social and recreational activities? What portion of your discretionary hours" is dedicated to evangelism, service to members in the body of Christ, and mission concern for the deprived and oppressed?

While serving with a large downtown church in the Midwest, I went to visit a couple who had attended a service the previous Sunday. They lived in a mobile home and had not been in the city long. They were not home when I called, but the next-door neighbor invited me in to tell me about them. The neighbor was not a Christian, but she knew of the couple's visits to various churches as they looked for a place to worship and serve regularly, and she could tell me what they had concluded.

The couple had decided not to become members of the downtown church because, as the neighbor explained it, that church already had a lot of qualified people to teach and serve. They chose instead a small church made up almost entirely of people from the working-class population of the city, many of whom had only recently arrived or were out of work. Here they felt they could be more useful. The wife sewed clothes for children and taught the women to sew. The husband used his free time to help others in the church find jobs.

As I listened to the neighbor relate the influence of this couple not only on the small church they had joined but also on the neighborhood where they lived, I realized that I, like perhaps many others, had never thought of a "good church" as one which provided such practical opportunities for service. I moved from that city shortly thereafter, and I never met this couple. But someday, when the Lord Jesus allows us to share with all the saints the blessings of his fellowship, I want to look them up and shake their hands.

What Must I Do?

A value system is useless unless it is "worked out within the culture and humdrum of everyday life."[6] So where do we start?

Jesus gives us the answer: "Seek first his kingdom and his righteousness, and all these things will be given to you as well" (Mt 6:33). Such seeking involves a basic attitude, a commitment to take on God's character and to know him and represent him in all aspects of our lives. First, it implies setting apart a specific time in order to get to know him. What kind of relationship would a husband and wife have if they just had a gen-

eral commitment to each other, but never talked to each other
or saw each other? We as Christians will include in our day and
week and year times to read the Bible, pray and worship, both
individually and corporately.

Second, we will seek to serve Christ, obeying his commands
and ministering to people. This will involve those closest to us,
our family, other Christians and the needy in general. "As we
have opportunity *[kairos]*, let us do good to all people, especially to those who belong to the family of believers" (Gal 6:10).
Such opportunities are everywhere around us. How much of
our time goes toward taking advantage of them?

Third, we are to be constantly involved in some form of
evangelism, what Jesus called "making disciples" (Mt 28:19).
This is a more comprehensive term than just "witnessing."
The imperative in the Great Commission is not to "go" but
rather to "make disciples" *(mathēteusate)*. The word for "go"
(poreuthentes) is a gerund, and in English it would be translated
literally "going." As such it cannot be the principal verb in the
sentence. A better translation would be "Wherever you go,
make disciples" or "While you are going, make disciples." The
geographical or temporal aspect is subservient to the principal
activity. Jesus understood that people were always "on the go";
there was no need to command *that*. But what is our main
priority in our going? That is the issue. And the answer is to
make disciples.

At this point we must stop to ask ourselves: does the use of
our time reflect our priorities? Do my priorities reflect the concern of Jesus for his church and the world? A vague "Well, I
suppose I could improve" isn't going to get us very far. But
here we can use one of the tools of time management: a time
log. Using this tool, we simply write down how we actually
spend our allotment of hours in any given day.

If you wish to try the method, you need to carry with you a
small notebook, previously marked off in reasonable intervals.
Very time-conscious people sometimes use six-minute intervals, because it makes it easier for them to evaluate their activi-

ties as percentages of an hour. You might try fifteen-minute segments. Length of interval is arbitrary, but it should be a good basic unit. Every hour or so you write down what you actually did in that time period. Do not wait until evening to fill in the time blanks; the whole purpose of the exercise is to get the facts before our memory has had a chance to blur them. Do this for enough days to get a reasonably accurate picture of your actual time usage.

The exercise may prove harder than you think. You may want to complain that this isn't a typical week, or you may find yourself fitting in something "spiritual" just so it will appear on the chart. Students have been known to embellish their charts for the benefit of the teacher. But there is no need for deception. All the time log does is to identify how you actually spend your chronological time.

Just a quick look through their marked days often helps people recognize that they have some illusions about their time usage. For example, many people think that their time is wasted by external forces when in reality it is their own lack of decision which allows the external forces to dominate their time. Many people think they have a lot of "discretionary time," that is, time they can dispose of as they wish. In reality, just the business of living takes up all but a small part of our time (this is especially true in less efficient, non-Western countries). This makes it all the more important to know what we are to do with that precious time rather than lose it by default.

Looking over your time logs with an eye to your basic goals as a Christian, you will want to consider changes, what the Bible calls "repentance." For a few people it may mean a radical change, such as changing jobs because they are not in a place where they can make any meaningful progress toward the goals of the kingdom. But for most of us it will mean identifying the opportunities which are daily passing us by. For almost everyone it will mean eliminating those time fillers which contribute nothing at all toward reaching our objectives as Christians, and instead seeking the Spirit's guidance for shaping a more ministering lifestyle.

Doing God's Ministry in God's Time

Moses is an example of someone who was filling his time with some very good activities and yet was not obeying the priorities which God had given him. It took his father-in-law, Jethro, to point out that "you cannot handle it alone" (Ex 18:18). He focused Moses on his main responsibilities and proposed that the remaining tasks should be done by other people (vv. 20-23). The incident sets a classic biblical precedent for delegation and illustrates that God is not at odds with good management.

Neither was Jesus. Jesus knew his basic purposes and fulfilled what he came to do (Jn 17), but he never appeared rushed or without time for unscheduled interruptions along the way (Mk 5). When sending out the Twelve, as recorded in Mark 6:7-12 and 30-32, we can see that Jesus knew and practiced the basic principles of training others. He taught and personally demonstrated what he wanted the disciples to do, sent them out to do it themselves and provided time for evaluation and encouragement.

The story of Gert Behanna's conversion illustrates how people can discover their own priorities as they discover God's. When she reached the point where she was completely without direction as a person and as a woman, Gert turned to God:

> I started from scratch. I prayed, "Our Father who art—." Then I stopped. *Our* Father—not theirs,—*ours.* Suddenly I was a sister to everybody. Suddenly I thought about my own sex. With the thought of women, I thought about cooking, which I knew nothing about. Calling my book dealer in Chicago, I said, "Mr. Chandler, I want a Bible and a copy of *The Joy of Cooking.*"
>
> "My God, what's happened to you?" asked Mr. Chandler.
>
> "My God has happened to me," I said. And He had.[7]

Perhaps the most practical book for showing the relationship of management tools for time control to the Christian's God-given goals comes not from a business executive but from a homemaker, Pat King. She is a modern Martha who has learned that to sit with Mary at Jesus' feet is not a waste of time. As a mother of ten (10!) she suffered more acutely than most the exhaustion of motherhood, but she still felt the pressure to do more than "just" care for children:

Therein lies the misery. There is so much we want to do, so much needing to be done in this world of ours, so much that society insists that we must do. We must not have ring-around-the-collar, we must have floors that gleam until we can see our faces in them, we must have furniture that reflects an arranged bouquet in living color. We must cook gourmet meals, be publicly aware, socially active, academically current.[8]

No matter how organized she was, she simply could not do all that was expected of her.

The misery ended, she says, when she saw that using time management skills is not the first step to getting order in our lives. First we must recognize that time (both *chronos* and *kairos*) is a gift from God, and that his priorities can always be fulfilled in the amount of time we have been given. With this perspective she found a great freedom, a release from "the expectations of the magazines." To do God's will did not mean meeting every request that school, church or civic groups proposed. "Instead, it means discerning in my heart what I've been called to do and saying no to what I haven't been called to."[9]

King recognizes that God is lavish with his gifts, so that there is always enough time to do what Jesus calls us to do. If we feel a schedule crunch, we can ask him for help and he will arrange the time we truly need. When things do not go according to schedule, there is a reason for it. This alerts us to the opportunities which, in human terms, come from things not working out as planned. "When we drop our lists and change our plans for His work, an amazing thing happens. Because God is never outdone in generosity He more than makes up for the time we've given. Almost miraculously everything on our lists get [sic] done anyway."[10]

If this approach sounds a bit mystical, let me add that King is not at all negative toward using management tools as the *second* step. She uses planning methods which any of us could use. For example, she understands "planning backwards" as a way to see the intermediate steps necessary to complete a complicated task. Planning backwards also helps to estimate more realistically how much time will be necessary to get the job done. By focusing our attention on the main goal, it helps us identify the low priority items in our schedules.

King also sees the value of knowing our "prime time," the periods when we function best. In those precious periods we schedule those responsibilities that demand the most of us. Conversely there are times of the day, week or year when we know that events press in around us and we should avoid, as much as possible, putting high priority tasks in those periods. She is aware, too, of the importance of temperament and bodily limitations on our attitude toward time.[11] One of her most helpful chapters deals with the effect of irritation and depression on our ability to respond to God's will because the Enemy uses these to sap our motivation. "One of the great thieves of our time is a lack of energy, for time has no value if we cannot use it."[12]

Putting her life in order, however, is not itself the end, but is rather the means of freeing her to serve people. She says with laughable understatement, "Maybe in regard to people, it's good to plan to be flexible."[13] In this, she shares the admirable perspective of the wife of a university professor in São Paulo, Brazil, who would do her shopping early in the morning in order to do missionary work later. But if she met a friend in the street market, she would stop to visit leisurely as if she had nothing else to do all day. She explained that if God put the missionary work earlier than she had planned, then he would undoubtedly leave time later for her domestic responsibilities. Time spent in God's service is not lost; it is merely rearranged. Our pocket planners make sense only as we "devote ourselves to the good deeds for which God has designed us" (Eph 2:10 NEB).

Lord, I have time.
I have plenty of time.
All the time that you give me,
The years of my life,
The days of my years,
The hours of my days,
They are all mine.
Mine to fill, quietly, calmly,
But to fill completely, up to the brim,
To offer them to you, that of their insipid water
You may make a rich wine as you
Made once in Cana of Galilee.[14]

8. Planning in the Quiet Time

Fighting time is a habit that can be broken.
LAWRENCE WRIGHT, CLOCKWORK MAN

Christians will usually seem to have a lot of time: you will wonder where it comes from.
C. S. LEWIS, MERE CHRISTIANITY

On my calendar there are but two days: today and That Day.
MARTIN LUTHER

For many years my private devotional life was like a small boy's piano practice: it was reserved for a certain hour of the day and performed with a determined exercise of the will, with hopes of achieving great things in a hurry. After a while the results did not seem to be worth the effort, and I became discouraged. Then any excuse would do to avoid that dull and repetitious exercise. Extra homework or a test at school, a vacation period, a stuffy nose—any change in the routine was enough to justify shortening or eliminating my quiet time with God.

Like piano practice, my quiet time was separated from the rest of the day by an arbitrary division of time. It was an isolated religious exercise of reading verses out of context and without application, and praying vague, general prayers on "spiritual" subjects. For a while, I found "just the thing" in prepared quiet-time guides, especially those designed for busy people. There would be a Scripture verse (or sometimes only a portion of a verse), a short commentary or story illustrating the text, and then a sentence prayer. The whole thing would take only four minutes. It was like aerobic exercise to someone who dislikes sports, offering the benefits of physical exercise in exchange for enduring a few minutes of prescribed exertion each day.

Such a quiet time may have its value as a form of sacrifice offered to the Lord and may also provide a seed thought for reflection through the day. But basically it remains isolated from the concerns of our normal daily activities. What we read or pray will rarely have a direct bearing on how we use our time. My personal planning and time management included space for a quiet time, but the quiet time did not contribute to my planning or time management.

Let's see what happens when we turn the process around. If in our quiet time we include a time for planning, we can orient our whole day (or a longer period) out of our time with God, instead of trying to find a few moments to squeeze him in. By including planning as part of our devotional life, (1) our devotions are not separated from the rest of our activities, (2) our planning is done in the context of the Word and prayer, (3) we affirm constantly our commitment to the purpose and values of the kingdom of God, and (4) we experience the guidance of the Holy Spirit in the establishing of our priorities and plans.

Liturgy and Life in Luther

Walter Trobisch has outlined this way of letting our life be organized in his booklet *Martin Luther's Quiet Time,* in which he shows that godly time planning is not really a new method at all. Luther explained his own devotional habits in a long letter to his barber, published in 1535 with the title *A Simple Way to Pray, for a Good Friend*. Trobisch interprets Luther to modern Christians in a way which shows the inherent unity of liturgy and life.[1]

At first glance, Luther's quiet time does not seem to be in any way extraordinary. He included those elements of devotion which we normally associate with a quiet time (Bible study and prayer), and he urged that meditation on the Scriptures be a guide to our prayers. He suggested that as we read a passage of Scripture (and it need not be a long one), we begin by asking questions. This stimulates active study because we are looking for something, not just letting the ideas flow by. Also, we need a notebook handy because when we find what we are looking for, we don't want to let it get away. "The weakest ink is more enduring than the strongest memory."

What questions should I ask myself? First, suggests Luther, ask, "What am I grateful for?" That is, what *in the text* leads me to thanksgiving? Then, concerning the same text, ask, "What do I regret, or what makes me sad?" In this way I identify with my spiritual ancestors in confession. Third, ask if the text does not lead me to intercede, either for myself or for others. Finally I should ask, "What am I to do?" The Bible is not just to be read but also to be obeyed. "Do not merely listen to the word, and so deceive yourselves. Do what it says" (Jas 1:22). The first two questions focus attention on our relationship with God our Father: thanksgiving and confession. The second pair of questions deals with our response to him in daily life: intercession and obedience.

In practice, our thoughts will not stay limited to the text we are studying, but even distractions may become a part of devotion. We will want to thank God for events and people in our lives that have little or nothing to do with the passage itself. Likewise, we will want to confess sins that do not appear in the passage we are reading at the moment. And there are certainly things happening in the world which make us sad, even though we were not directly involved in them. We may bring before God the sins, or the consequences of sins, of our family, neighborhood and nation. So the final step is to use the same questions which we used for the Bible text, this time asking ourselves what other things we can thank God for, confess or pray about.

As we pray for ourselves and our world, we put into practice a doctrine long defended but frequently misunderstood, the doctrine of the priesthood of all believers. One aspect of this doctrine is certainly that we have direct access to God the Father with no intermediary but Jesus Christ. It is a tremendous privilege to be invited to approach the throne of God directly, and we must never take it for granted. But the other part of this privilege is the responsibility to intercede for others. Because we do have access to the Father, we must exercise our priestly function by bringing others into the heavenly places. By intercession, we have a part in God's work throughout the world.

The revolutionary aspect of this devotional plan lies in the fourth question; What should I do? This question links our quiet time to how we plan to use the following hours and days. No longer can quiet time be a strictly spiritual exercise. Instead, the quiet time becomes a family council, a huddle, a board meeting; that is, it becomes a time to be with the Father who is also our Guide and Boss. Since he is the one who knows the future, has given purpose to our lives and included us in the mission of his church, we can expect that our "to do" list will come out of our time with him.

Guidance: Your Quiet Time and Time Usage

How does this happen? First, the text we are reading may point out specific things to be done. A missionary, who suffered from terrible headaches that kept her from fulfilling her assignments, was convicted by the Holy Spirit about harboring anger against her colleagues through her reading of Ephesians

4:25-26: "Therefore each of you must put off falsehood and speak truthfully to his neighbor, for we are all members of one body. 'In your anger do not sin': Do not let the sun go down while you are still angry." For her the application was to deal with her anger toward others on a day-to-day basis. Part of her evening devotions from then on included a time of evaluation to see if she had dealt honestly and openly with other team members; and if she discovered anything "left over," she would deal with it immediately, before the day was over. As long as she followed the biblical injunction, she was free from her headaches and became a valued contributor to the mission effort.

Other times, the Spirit may bring to mind someone or some task which normally we would not have thought of. Like Ananias who was instructed to visit Saul (Acts 9:10-19), we may be led to include in our plans things we would otherwise have known nothing about, or certainly avoided if we had known. Like Ananias, too, we often resist these ideas since they appear unreasonable or risky, but that reticence usually only suggests how different from God's is our idea of how the kingdom should be managed!

On one occasion, the "to do" list which emerged from my quiet time was long and complicated, involving a lot of running around, since we were without a telephone; yet I felt compelled to schedule it all in the morning, leaving my afternoon free. I was puzzled, wondering why my morning looked so crowded while the afternoon remained blank. As it turned out, all the planned activities of the morning fell into place more quickly than usual, and right after lunch a friend from out of town stopped by to visit, spending the entire afternoon with us before resuming his travels. The God who knows our future and our limitations makes time for us when we need it.

This kind of guidance seems mystical and subject to abuse, and it is. The devil can disguise his voice to sound like the Holy Spirit, and the Christian can be easily misled. Many times I confuse my own interests with what I think God wants me to do. More than once I have felt certain that I urgently needed to talk with someone, only to discover that that person was out of town. Such experiences are a good check on what could become a kind of magic.

We should not think that direct guidance is common. God did not normally speak to Ananias directly, as recorded in Acts, but on one occasion he did. I wholeheartedly agree with rational approaches to guidance, such as those suggested in Alan Redpath's *Getting to Know the Will of God,* Paul Little's *Affirming the Will of God* and Garry Friesen's *Decision Making and the Will of God,* yet there are too many witnesses to God's occasional direct leading for us to reject it. Certainly, as we learn to discern the Spirit's voice we can walk confidently in his guidance, even if that means keeping our schedules more open.

One of the most intriguing aspects of discovering through our devotional life freedom from the tyranny of the urgent comes not from finding out what we are to do, but from learning what we are *not* supposed to do. Besides priorities (those things which we should, by all means, do), there are what Peter Drucker calls "posteriorities," those things which must be avoided or eliminated if we are to accomplish our priorities. A great sense of freedom comes from discovering that something we thought had to be done really doesn't, or from consciously putting aside some nagging task until an hour when we can deal with it.

Of course, most of our time is concerned with normal day-to-day responsibilities: our family, work, church and so on. Most of our guidance will concern them, too. Thoughts about these "things to do" often intrude into our quiet time. Instead of trying to dismiss these thoughts as secular concerns from the devil meant to disrupt your spiritual devotions, take the time to write them down. This serves both to free your mind of them and also to determine your priorities, or identify your posteriorities. As you pray about each of these responsibilities, you can get a clearer idea of how each contributes to the kingdom of God.

Each Day Has Enough Trouble of Its Own 2/5513

When these questions become a daily pattern in your devotional life, each day becomes linked to the others. Did you do what was on yesterday's "to do" list? Yes? Then praise the Lord! No? Then make it a part of your confession today. And what remains from yesterday's list may become a part of your "do today" list.

Why didn't you do what was on your list for yesterday? You may discover that you simply had too much to do, or that you underestimated how much time certain activities would take. You may have been guilty of adding to your day activities that others can do, or which you think others expect of you, or which you included in your list, hoping that God would eventually approve. Most people who have a time problem do not need a management course to enable them to do more. They are already doing too much and need to limit their commitments. Your quiet time may be showing you that you need to say "no" more often to those who make demands on your time.

In any case, what happened yesterday becomes a matter for your next "family council." Such daily huddles with the Father give us the short-term direction we need for daily living. We review past performance, check our direction and get new marching orders. This kind of quiet time is a concrete way to "seek first the kingdom of God"; and the result is that we see the remaining "all these things" get put in proper perspective and we reduce our concern for the future (Mt 6:33-34). Most freeing of all for our inner time, we can deal with guilt on a regular and concrete basis.

There is no reason the same integrated view of devotion and life cannot apply to longer periods of time. The same Spirit who can direct our steps today can also help us deal with next week or next year. Alan Redpath, for example, describes how God directed him into the pastoral ministry through his quiet time, but it was a process which took over a year.[2]

Major decisions like choosing our vocation, using our gifts, spending our money, and helping a child face problems—these are not up for review every day. Once we are on the right track of ministry and service in our lives, we need not be repeatedly making these same decisions. But when time for major decisions comes, we may need more than just our normal quiet time in order to gain the needed perspective. Tom Sine in *The Mustard Seed Conspiracy* has noted that much long-range planning by Christians is way off the mark because Christians have not paused long enough to see what changes God is bringing about, or because they did not relate their planning to the goals of the kingdom.[3] Check with the Lord in your next quiet time to see if he does not suggest separating some time specifically for an evaluation of your time and activity commitments. Lorne Sanny's *How to Spend a Day in Prayer* may be of help.

A quiet time need not be private; sharing with someone else is an important part of our devotional life no matter how we go about it. Especially in this quiet time plan, where decisions are being made and our time planned out, it is essential that we share with others who must coordinate *their* activities with us. God's family council is not just Father-daughter or Father-son; it includes brothers and sisters as well.

My wife, Beth, and I have experimented with Luther's quiet time for some years. We discovered early that we needed time each day to go over the day plan together. It was frustrating at first because it took so much *chronos* to see the *kairos* of the other. But patience has brought some beautiful experiences. Once, after a period of heavy ministry, I realized I needed to spend some time with Beth for more than just coordinating our activities. Into the morning plan went "Make arrangements for the kids to stay with neighbor after school," and I left the afternoon completely open. At breakfast, Beth looked perplexed.

"My quiet time was funny," she said. "I don't know what I'm supposed to do this afternoon."

I smiled. "I know. You're going out with me."

Sometimes, however, we came up with conflicting plans for

the day. Was one of us not hearing the voice of the Lord correctly? We found that there was no need to accuse one another of being unspiritual, and instead we set up a procedure to resolve such seeming contradictions. If we had a serious conflict of time, one we could not resolve between the two of us, we felt that someone else in the church was supposed to be involved. So we would call around, asking, "Can you babysit on Friday?" "Can you take the Bible study next week?" "Can you make a hospital visit?" Rarely has it been necessary for either of us to renounce completely one of our important plans. But if it comes to that, then we recognize the impasse as an opportunity to "submit to one another out of reverence for Christ" (Eph 5:21). In this context, the following verse, "Wives, submit to your husbands as to the Lord," carries no idea of marital power struggles. Submission, by either husband or wife, is not defeat, but rather it is to "understand what the Lord's will is" (Eph 5:17)!

Being Built into a Spiritual Home
Ideally, this is the pattern for an entire church. The values and the goals of the kingdom are not just for a few but for everyone. Planning should go on in the devotional life of all its members and in its corporate sharing. As God sifts our priorities, eliminating unnecessary and unproductive activities, we will discover we have time for ministry. As others in the body become involved, they will call upon still others. Thus the church as a whole becomes a model of the kingdom, exhibiting God's sense of timing in its body life of community, outreach and service. The work of ministry is shared, not accumulated on a few "professionals." The entire church becomes a community living in God's time instead of just a group of people who worship in the same building on Sundays.

At first, your notebook will not fill up quickly. Lists of thanksgivings and confessions will be short and your prayer lists limited to a few people close to you. It is hard to see God's grace operating behind all expressions of good in the world, or to admit complicity in the woes of peoples far away. But through discipline (writing) and perseverance (writing!), your list will grow. Soon it may get to the point where it seems ridiculous to fill so many notebooks with small blessings and sins. But it is not ridiculous at all. It means that your capacity for thankfulness and repentance, for true joy and sorrow, is increasing. Christians never tire of God's promise to "forgive us our sins and purify us from all unrighteousness" (1 Jn 1:9), nor of expressing gratitude for his undeserved favor toward us.

In the same way, a church will at first be slow in reaching out to the needy world or in serving one another in concrete ways. It is especially hard if the church is in a community which appears to have all it needs—and more—and if the suffering world is thought to be an ocean away. Part of the American heritage of self-reliance makes it difficult to admit that we have needs or that we should offer to alleviate situations which are "none of our business." "We're not desperate yet," remarked a man whose family was experiencing health and job problems. Why do we need to be desperate before we allow others to serve us? Or why do we allow others to become desperate before we think we can offer to help? Instead, to the extent that a church, or a mission group of a church, assumes the goals of the kingdom and reaffirms its priorities through its devotional life, it will give proportionally more time to meeting the needs of people and less to establishing and maintaining programs.

Before long, a pattern emerges in the use of our time. We reveal a style of ministry according to our gifts, and in a healthy church our gifts complement others' "so that the body of Christ may be built up." These spiritual gifts are not divorced from natural talents or personality, because it is the same God who "graces" us with both our natural inheritance and also the supernatural means of ministry.[4] Therefore, when future-oriented, choleric people dedicate themselves to the goals of the kingdom, they may show strong gifts in leadership or administration. Similarly a sanguine person may reveal the gift of mercy in a way that other temperaments may not.

Time becomes an ally in the kingdom, not an enemy. It is a gift to gifted people. We don't need to try to suspend or delay time's passage. In fact, because the goals of the kingdom are relational, time brings insight, wisdom and experience to be shared and valued. As God's people dedicate their gifts, including time, to the furtherance of the kingdom, individual personality and even culture exhibit the marks of redemption, and the signs of the new community emerge in a people whose time has come and is about to arrive.

9. Timely Conclusions

Though I am always in haste, I am never in a hurry, because I never undertake more work than I can go through with calmness of spirit.
JOHN WESLEY

In the long run it is not the years in your life but the life in your years that counts.
ADLAI STEVENSON

We live in memory, decision and hope, elements of our personality which correspond to the external past, present and future. The link between this external time and our inner life is in our temperament, or, as Sören Kierkegaard expressed it, our very selves are "tensed." Time takes on meaning in view of who we are.[1]

When, in Christ, we experience God's time (what the Bible calls "eternal life"), we join his adventure in the world. We take part in the creation that begins from within, not as a form of "timelessness" but rather of "timefulness" (2 Cor 4:13-16; Rom 6:4). We join now in what God has been doing and will continue to do for ages. Only in this sense can we understand such apparent inversions of time as we see in Revelation 13:8, "the Lamb that was slain from the creation of the world"; or the paradox of prayer implied in Isaiah 65:24, "Before they call I will answer"; or our identification with the sins of our forefathers outlined by Paul in Romans 5, "Just as sin entered the world through one man, and death through sin, and in this way death came to all men, because all sinned," We can also learn to experience God's sense of timing and his eternal rest in the midst of our present activity.

We may experience this personally in a realistic devotional life. The spiritual and the secular meet where God directs us in seeking first his kingdom, and the result is the "insecure stability" of living by faith. Those who become accustomed to God's timing say with the psalmist, "My times are in your hands"; they enjoy calmness of spirit knowing that God is in control of events, and they also find it exciting to see the fresh, unplanned events which God brings into their lives.

When a family, a cell group or a church gets this sense of God's *kairos,* the witness to his redemptive grace becomes all the more vivid and compelling. God's church becomes an "Easter people," living signs of the new community which God is even now forming. Such communities are not dominated by the natural temperaments of a few of their members, nor are they squeezed into the mold of the dominant temperament of their society. In the case of a triumphalistic culture, as in North America, for example, the church's priorities are not determined by the plans proposed or imposed by a materialistic vision of the future; instead such groups bring Christ's healing message from the past to bear on the present and to warn of the coming judgment on the history we are now making. In an event-oriented society it means that the church's stewardship before God is not perverted by those with status and power; its present is characterized by justice, righting the wrongs of the past and opening the future for those who otherwise will have none.

In either case the biblical culture becomes our model. Not that we go back to the particulars of that age, but that we reform ourselves in light of the Scriptures instead of judging biblical views of time and personality as primitive or outmoded. The biblical culture was future oriented in that it saw an end toward which history was moving, with events taking their significance according to that end. There would be triumph, but triumphalism was inappropriate because the triumph would arrive through suffering and sacrifice.

Biblical culture was also event oriented in that the sequence or haste with which the future arrived was not primary. Present events have their own sense of completeness and make their unique contribution to the end of history. And each event has its own opportunity, which demands choices and decisions based on our view of the eschatological goal. "Now is the time of God's favor, now is the day of salvation" (2 Cor 6:2b).

The world is only now waking up to its own apocalyptic alarm clock. The time is short, and panic is sure to set in soon. But the church has long been aware that "our salvation is nearer now than when we first believed. The night is nearly over; the day is almost here" (Rom 13:11-12). The church need not lose its head with those around it. Instead, it must point confidently and joyfully to the sunrise. God will see to it that his Son's bride gets to the wedding on time.

Notes

Chapter 1: The Time of Your Life

[1]Augustine *The Confessions* 11.13. Einstein, contradicting the Newtonian view of time, wrote, "If we assume that all matter would disappear from the world, then, before relativity, one believed that space and time would continue existing in an empty world. But, according to the theory of relativity, if matter and its motion disappeared, there would no longer be any space or time" (Quoted in Philipp Frank, *Einstein, His Life and Times* [New York: Knopf, 1947], p. 178).

[2]Simon John DeVries, *Yesterday, Today and Tomorrow* (Grand Rapids: Eerdmans, 1975), p. 38.

[3]"The week was unknown to early civilizations. . . . The week, the hour and the subdivisions of the hour are all artificial because no week or hour is separated from another by any natural event, like the daily sun or the monthly moon" (Lawrence Wright, *Clockwork Man* [New York: Horizon Press, 1969], p. 15). See also Niels-Erik Andreasen, *The Christian Use of Time* (Nashville: Abingdon, 1978), p. 25.

[4]Hernâni Donato, *História do Calendário* (São Paulo: Edições Melhoramentos, 1976), p. 64.

[5]Robert H. Schuller, *Move Ahead with Possibility Thinking* (Old Tappan, N.J.: Fleming H. Revell, 1973), p. 116.

[6]Quoted in George Sullivan, "Time: How to Squeeze the Most Out of It," *TWA Ambassador,* November 1977, p. 22.

[7]*Philadelphia Associated Press,* 13 March 1977, quoted in Richard Bolles, *The Three Boxes of Life* (Berkeley: Ten Speed Press, 1978), p. 265.

[8]J. B. Priestley, *Man and Time* (London: Aldus Books, 1964), p. 66.

[9]Ibid.

[10]Peter Cohen, *The Gospel According to the Harvard Business School* (Garden City, N.Y.: Doubleday, 1973), p. 328.

[11]Benjamin Franklin, *The Way to Wealth,* 7 July 1757.

[12]Larry L. Rasmussen, *Economic Anxiety and Christian Faith* (Minneapolis: Augsburg, 1981), p. 40.

[13]Andrew Kirk, "The Kingdom, the Church and a Distressed World," *Evangelical Review of Theology* 5 (1981), p. 75.

[14]Peter L. Berger, *Pyramids of Sacrifice* (Garden City, N.Y.: Doubleday, 1976), p. 234.

[15]Eugene Peterson, "The Unbusy Pastor," *Leadership* 2, no. 3 (Summer 1981): 70; italics added for clarity.

Chapter 2: Time and Temperament

[1]J. T. Fraser, ed., *The Voices of Time* (New York: G. Braziller, 1966), p. xix.

[2]Jim Davidson, *Effective Time Management* (New York: Human Sciences Press, 1978), p. 7.

[3]Bolles, *Three Boxes,* pp. 142-43.

[4]Priestley, *Man and Time,* p. 66.

[5]A. Moneim El-Meligi, "A Technique for Exploring Time Experiences in Mental Disorders," in *The Future of Time,* ed. Henri Yaker, Humphrey Osmond and Frances Cheek (Garden City, N.Y.: Doubleday, 1971).

[6]Harriet Mann, Miriam Siegler and Humphrey Osmond, "Psychotypology of Time," in *The Future of Time,* Yaker et al. This article includes some excellent examples of psychological types, with relation to their time orientation, from classical literature. Tim LaHaye has popularized the relationship between the temperaments and Christian faith. See his *Spirit-Controlled Temperament, Transformed Temperaments* and *Understanding the Male Temperament.*

[7]See Ole Hallesby, *Temperament and the Christian Faith* (Minneapolis, Minn.: Augsburg, 1962) for a full, sympathetic treatment, including biblical examples.

[8]Ibid., p. 7.

[9]C. S. Lewis, *The Screwtape Letters* (Glasgow: William Collins Sons, 1979), p. 91.

[10]Edward T. Hall, *The Silent Language* (Garden City, N.Y.: Doubleday, 1959), p. 154; and Hall, *The Hidden Dimension* (Garden City, N.Y.: Doubleday, 1966), chap. 10. For a bibliography on time perception in intercultural understanding, see Jerry K. Frye, *Time: A Significant Variable of Intercul-*

tural Communication Research (Armidale, Australia: Communication Association of the Pacific, 1980).

[11]Rudyard Kipling, *The Naulahka,* in *Rudyard Kipling's Verse* (Garden City, N.Y.: Doubleday, Doran & Co., 1943), p. 537.

[12]John S. Mbiti, *New Testament Eschatology in an African Background* (London: Oxford Univ. Press, 1971), pp. 31ff.

[13]Marvin K. Mayers, *Christianity Confronts Culture* (Grand Rapids: Zondervan, 1974), p. 319.

[14]Vianna Moog, *Bandeirantes e Pioneiros* (Rio de Janeiro: Editora Globo, 1954), p. 357. My translation: *"O americano já não contempla; o americano já não reflete; o americano já não sabe descancar."*

Chapter 3: Telling Time in Tijuana

[1]José de Alencar, *Cinco Minutos,* 9th ed. (São Paulo: Edições Melhoramentos, 1962), p. 7.

[2]This classification is from Mayers, *Christianity Confronts Culture,* p. 159.

[3]Daniel Bell, *The Cultural Contradictions of Capitalism* (New York: Basic Books, 1976), p. 90.

[4]John Mbiti, *New Testament Eschatology,* p. 29.

[5]Marvin K. Mayers, *A Look at Latin American Lifestyles* (Dallas: SIL Museum of Anthropology, 1976), p. 90.

[6]Mayers, *Christianity Confronts Culture,* pp. 151-52.

[7]These images are drawn from Ross A. Webber, *Time Is Money!* (New York: The Free Press, 1980), pp. 3-4.

[8]Hall, *Silent Language,* p. 156.

[9]David J. Hesselgrave, *Communicating Christ Cross-Culturally* (Grand Rapids: Zondervan, 1978), p. 281. Hesselgrave's emphasis.

[10]Robert J. Maxwell, "Anthropological Perspectives," in *The Future of Time,* Yaker et al., p. 55.

[11]Moog, *Bandeirantes e Pioneiros,* p. 336.

[12]Mayers, *A Look at Latin American Lifestyles,* p. 43. See chaps. 3 and 4 for an excellent discussion on "status" and "the behavior of status."

[13]David L. Szanton, "Cultural Confrontation in the Philippines," in *Cultural Frontiers of the Peace Corps,* ed. Robert B. Textor (Cambridge, Mass.: MIT Press, 1966), p. 43.

[14]Mbiti, *New Testament Eschatology,* p. 61.

[15]Cited in Mayers, *Christianity Confronts Culture,* p. 114.

[16]Ian M. Fraser, *The Fire Runs* (London: SCM, 1975), p. 4.

[17]Eugene A. Nida, *Customs and Cultures* (New York: Harper and Row, 1954), chap. 9: "Old Customs and New Ways."

[18]Quoted by Donald Johnson in "Leadership Readiness of the American Indian," in *Christian Leadership in Indian America,* ed. Tom Claus and Dale

W. Keitzman (Chicago: Moody, 1976).

[19]Massaud Moisés, *A Criação Literária,* 6th ed. (São Paulo: Edições Melhoramentos, 1973), p. 201. My translation.

[20]Kosuke Koyama, *Three Mile an Hour God* (Maryknoll, N.Y.: Orbis, 1979), p. 54.

[21]Ibid., p. 7.

[22]Arthur C. Custance, *Time and Eternity* (Grand Rapids: Zondervan, 1977), p. 26.

Chapter 4: The Choleric Culture

[1]Quoted in Wright, *Clockwork Man,* p. 104.

[2]Alvin Toffler, *The Third Wave* (New York: Bantam Books, 1980), p. 52.

[3]G. T. Whitrow, *The Nature of Time* (Baltimore: Penguin Books, 1975), p. 19.

[4]Quoted in Wright, *Clockwork Man.*

[5]Toffler, p. 103.

[6]Arthur DeMoss and David Enlow, *How to Change Your World in 12 Weeks* (Tappan, N.J.: Fleming H. Revell, 1969), p. 58.

[7]Rasmussen, *Economic Anxiety,* p. 39.

[8]The phrase is from Michael Kinsley, "Workaholics Are Overdoing Time," *Detroit Free Press,* 15 August 1977, p. 13-A.

[9]For Peter Drucker's philosophy of management, see his *The Effective Executive* (1967) and *Management: Tasks, Responsibilities, Practices* (1974), both published by Harper and Row. For a highly touted appeal for transcendent values in business, see O. A. Ohmann, "Skyhooks: With Special Implications for Monday through Friday," *Harvard Business Review—On Management* (New York: Harper and Row, 1975). Ted W. Engstrom and Edward R. Dayton mention almost a dozen secular management experts and conclude, "It has been fascinating over a period of years to watch secular management theorists come closer and closer to the New Testament model of the church as an organization" *(The Art of Management for Christian Leaders* [Waco, Tex.: Word, 1976], p. 101). For a cynical look at management training without a Christian value system, see Cohen, *The Gospel According to the Harvard Business School.*

[10]Engstrom and Dayton, *Art of Management,* pp. 37-39.

[11]Jacques Ellul, *The Presence of the Kingdom,* trans. Olive Wyon (New York: Seabury, 1967), pp. 88-89. Ellul's emphasis.

[12]Karen Mains, *Open Heart, Open Home* (Elgin, Ill.: David C. Cook, 1976), pp. 166-67.

[13]Edward R. Dayton, "Toward a Theology of Management," *Leadership* 2, no. 4 (Fall 1981):46.

[14]Marya Mannes, "Time, Gentlemen, Please," quoted in Speed B. Leas, *Time Management* (Nashville: Abingdon, 1978), p. 34.

[15]Edward T. Hall, *Beyond Culture* (Garden City, N.Y.: Anchor Books, 1976), p. 18.

[16]Peter Drucker, *Managing for Results* (New York: Harper and Row, 1964), p. 173.

[17]Mann et al., "Psychotypology of Time" in *The Future of Man*, pp. 173-74.

[18]Wright, *Clockwork Man*, p. 236.

[19]Toffler, *Third Wave*, pp. 11-12.

[20]C. S. Lewis, *The Screwtape Letters* and *Screwtape Proposes a Toast* (New York: Macmillan, 1961), pp. 5-6.

[21]J. Stanley Glen, *Justification by Success* (Atlanta: John Knox, 1979), pp. 100-101. Chapter 5, "The Invisible Sin," and chapter 6, "The Sovereignty of the Invisible Religion," give his basic biblical argument and his concern for the unperceived influence of power on the mission of the church.

[22]Alan Lakein, *How to Get Control of Your Time and Your Life* (New York Peter H. Wyden, 1973), p. 3.

[23]Earl Jaboy, *The Kingdom of Self* (Plainfield, N.J.: Logos International, 1974), p. 72.

[24]Ellul, *Presence of the Kingdom*, pp. 11-12. Ellul's emphasis.

Chapter 5: The Kingdom of Opportunity

[1]Abraham Heschel, *The Sabbath* (New York: Farrar, Strauss and Young, 1951), p. 9. See also Niels-Erik Andreasen, *The Christian Use of Time* (Nashville: Abingdon, 1978), p. 25.

[2]Thorleif Boman, *Hebrew Thought Compared with Greek* (Philadelphia: Westminster, 1960), p. 128. See also Claude Tresmontant, *A Study of Hebrew Thought*, trans. Michael F. Gibson (New York: Desclee Co., 1960), p. 26, and Mark C. Taylor, "Time's Struggle with Space," *Harvard Theological Review* 66, no. 3 (July 1973): 314-15. Wright cites an interesting historical judgment by Thucydides from his introduction to the history of the Peloponnesian War: "Judging from the evidence which I am able to trust after most careful inquiry, I should imagine that former ages were not great, either in their wars or in anything else" (*Clockwork Man*, p. 23).

[3]James Barr, *Biblical Words for Time* (Naperville, Ill.: Alec R. Allenson, 1962), pp. 143-44.

[4]Hans-Christoph Hahn, "Time," in *The New International Dictionary of New Testament Theology*, ed. Colin Brown, 3 vols. (Grand Rapids: Zondervan, 1978), 3:826.

[5]Barr criticizes John Marsh, *The Fullness of Time*, J. A. T. Robinson, *In the End, God . . .* , and even Oscar Cullmann, *Christ and Time* (who may not be as deserving as the others) for this fault (Barr, *Biblical Words for Time*, pp. 26-50). The story is told of the Russian theologian, Nicolas Berdyaev, author of another book which minimizes the importance of chrono-

logical time, *The Beginning and the End,* that while he was delivering a paper in which he "pleaded passionately for the insignificance and unreality of time," he suddenly stopped and glanced anxiously at his watch, for fear that he might be a few minutes late in taking his medicine. The story is told in G. J. Whitrow, *The Nature of Time,* p. 134.

[6]Barr, *Biblical Words for Time,* pp. 51, 109.

[7]Discussed in Bolles, *Three Boxes of Life,* p. 31.

[8]Koyama, *Three Mile an Hour God,* p. 4.

[9]The suggestion comes from Paul Tillich, "Kairos," in *A Handbook of Christian Theology,* ed. Marvin Halverson (New York: Meridian Books, 1958), p. 194.

[10]John R. Wilch, *Time and Event* (Long Island City, N.Y.: E. J. Brill, 1969), p. 128.

[11]Andrew Kirk, "The Kingdom, the Church and a Distressed World," *Evangelical Review of Theology* 5, no. 1 (April 1981): 78.

[12]Samuel Escobar, "Beyond Liberation Theology: Evangelical Missiology in Latin America," *International Bulletin of Missionary Research* 6, no. 3 (July 1982): 111. See also Klaus Bockmuehl, *The Challenge of Marxism* (Downers Grove, Ill.: InterVarsity Press, 1980), pp. 17-20.

[13]C. T. McIntire, "The Focus of Historical Study: A Christian View," *Fides et Historia* 14, no. 1 (Fall-Winter 1981): 9.

[14]Donald M. MacKay, *Human Science and Human Dignity* (Downers Grove, Ill.: InterVarsity Press, 1979), p. 111.

[15]DeVries, *Yesterday, Today and Tomorrow,* p. 340.

Chapter 6: Taking the Pressure off Redemption

[1]Rebecca Manley Pippert, *Out of the Saltshaker* (Downers Grove, Ill.: Inter-Varsity Press, 1979), pp. 121-22.

[2]William Pannell, "Evangelism and Power," *Evangelical Review of Theology* 5, no. 1 (April 1981): 98. Pannell's emphasis.

[3]Ellul, *Presence of the Kingdom,* p. 11.

[4]Wilch, *Time and Event,* p. 127.

[5]Herbert M. Carson, "The Epistles of Paul to the Colossians and Philemon," in *Tyndale New Testament Commentaries,* ed. R. V. G. Tasker (Grand Rapids: Eerdmans, 1960), p. 97.

[6]DeVries, *Yesterday, Today and Tomorrow,* p. 53.

[7]Yaker, *Future of Time,* p. 33. Yaker's emphasis.

[8]Ada Lum, HIS magazine (January 1980), back cover.

Chapter 7: Seeking First the Future of God

[1]MacKay, *Human Science and Human Dignity,* pp. 115-16. MacKay's emphasis.

[2]This is the title of an excellent book on the nature and purpose of the church by Michael Griffiths.

[3]Kirk, "The Kingdom, the Church and a Distressed World," pp. 76, 90. For a more thorough discussion of these three elements of the kingdom and the relationship between them, see Waldron Scott, *Bring Forth Justice* (Grand Rapids: Eerdmans, 1980).

[4]Pannell, "Evangelism and Power," p. 100.

[5]Ibid., p. 97.

[6]Engstrom and Dayton, *Art of Management,* p. 218.

[7]Gert Behanna, *God Isn't Dead,* quoted in Jabay, *Kingdom of Self,* p. 84.

[8]Pat King, *How to Have All the Time You Need Every Day* (Wheaton, Ill.: Tyndale House, 1980), p. 49.

[9]Ibid., p. 61.

[10]Ibid., p. 85.

[11]See her chapter "Getting to Know Me" for down-to-earth descriptions of the four temperaments and their effect on time usage. She quotes with relish Dr. William Nolen: "If you will concede, as I will, that the most miserable person in the world is the woman in the grip of a severe attack of premenstrual tension, then you will also have to concede that the second most miserable person is whoever is closest to her" (from *McCall's,* February 1973, p. 12). Her conclusion: Plan for it!

[12]King, *How to Have All the Time,* p. 44.

[13]Ibid., p. 63.

[14]Michael Quoist, *Prayers* (Fairway, Kans.: Andrews & McMeel, 1974), p. 98.

Chapter 8: Planning in the Quiet Time

[1]Walter Trobisch, *Martin Luther's Quiet Time* (Downers Grove, Ill.: Inter-Varsity Press, 1975), p. 15.

[2]Alan Redpath, *Getting to Know the Will of God* (Downers Grove, Ill.: InterVarsity Press, 1954), p. 14.

[3]Tom Sine, *The Mustard Seed Conspiracy* (Waco, Tex.: Word, 1981), pp. 17-18.

[4]Michael Griffiths, *Grace-Gifts* (Grand Rapids: Eerdmans, 1979), pp. 69-71. See also Stephen F. Winward, *Fruit of the Spirit* (Leicester, England: Inter-Varsity Press, 1981), pp. 50-52; and John R. W. Stott, *Baptism and Fullness,* 2nd ed. (Downers Grove, Ill.: InterVarsity Press, 1976), pp. 90-94.

Chapter 9: Timely Conclusions

[1]Referred to in Taylor, "Time's Struggle with Space," p. 329.

Bibliography

General

Alencar, José de. *Cinco Minutos.* 9th ed. São Paulo: Edições Melhoramentos, 1962.

Augustine. *The Confessions.* Translated by R. S. Pine-Coffin. New York: Penguin Books, 1961.

Bell, Daniel. *The Cultural Contradictions of Capitalism.* Basic Books, 1976.

Berger, Peter L. *Pyramids of Sacrifice.* Garden City, N.Y.: Doubleday, 1976.

Bolles, Richard N. *The Three Boxes of Life.* Berkeley: Ten Speed Press, 1978.

Donato, Hernâni. *História do Calendário.* São Paulo: Edições Melhoramentos, 1976.

Fraser, Ian M. *The Fire Runs.* London: SCM, 1975.

Jaboy, Earl. *The Kingdom of Self.* Plainfield, N.J.: Logos International, 1974.

Lewis, C. S. *The Screwtape Letters* and *Screwtape Proposes a Toast.* New York: Macmillan, 1961.

Little, Paul E. *Affirming the Will of God.* Downers Grove, Ill.: InterVarsity Press, 1971.

MacKay, Donald M. *Human Science and Human Dignity.* Downers Grove, Ill.: InterVarsity Press, 1979.

Mains, Karen Burton. *Open Heart, Open Home.* Elgin, Ill.: David C. Cook, 1976.

Moisés, Massaud. *A Criação Literária*. 6th ed. São Paulo: Edições Melhoramentos, 1973.

Rasmussen, Larry L. *Economic Anxiety and Christian Faith*. Minneapolis: Augsburg, 1981.

Redpath, Alan. *Getting to Know the Will of God*. Downers Grove, Ill.: InterVarsity Press, 1954.

Schuller, Robert H. *Move Ahead with Possibility Thinking*. Old Tappan, N.J.: Fleming H. Revell, 1973.

Tresmontant, Claude. *A Study of Hebrew Thought*. Translated by Michael F. Gibson. New York: Desclee Co., 1960.

The Biblical View of Time

Andreasen, Niels-Erik. *The Christian Use of Time*. Nashville: Abingdon, 1978.

Barr, James. *Biblical Words for Time*. Naperville, Ill.: Alec R. Allenson, Inc.; London: SCM, 1962.

Boman, Thorheif. *Hebrew Thought Compared with Greek*. Philadelphia: Westminster, 1960.

Carson, Herbert M. *The Epistles of Paul to the Colossians and Philemon*. Tyndale New Testament Commentaries. Edited by R. V. G. Tasker. Grand Rapids: Eerdmans, 1960.

Cullmann, Oscar. *Christ and Time*. Rev. ed. Translated by Floyd V. Filson. Philadelphia: Westminster, 1964.

DeVries, Simon John. *Yesterday, Today and Tomorrow*. Grand Rapids: Eerdmans, 1975.

Hahn, Hans-Christoph, "Time." In *The New International Dictionary of New Testament Theology*. Edited by Colin Brown. 3 vols. Grand Rapids: Zondervan, 1978.

Heschel, Abraham. *The Sabbath*. New York: Farrar, Strauss and Young, 1951.

Tillich, Paul, "Kairos." In *A Handbook of Christian Theology*. Edited by Marvin Halverson. New York: Meridian Books, 1958.

Wilch, John R. *Time and Event*. Long Island City, N.Y.: E. J. Brill, 1969.

The Church and the Kingdom

Ellul, Jacques. *The Presence of the Kingdom*. Translated by Olive Wyon. New York: Seabury, 1967.

Escobar, Samuel. "Beyond Liberation Theology: Evangelical Missiology in Latin America." *International Bulletin of Missionary Research* 6 (1982): 100-14.

Glen, J. Stanley. *Justification by Success*. Atlanta: John Knox, 1979.

Griffiths, Michael. *Grace-Gifts*. Grand Rapids: Eerdmans, 1979.

Kirk, J. Andrew. "The Kingdom, the Church and a Distressed World."

Evangelical Review of Theology 5 (1981).

Moltmann, Jürgen, *Hope and Planning*. Translated by Margaret Clarkson. New York: Harper and Row, 1971.

Pannell, William E. "Evangelism and Power." *Evangelical Review of Theology* 5 (1981).

Pippert, Rebecca Manley. *Out of the Saltshaker*. Downers Grove, Ill.: InterVarsity Press, 1979.

Scott, Waldron. *Bring Forth Justice*. Grand Rapids: Eerdmans, 1980.

Stott, John R. W. *Baptism and Fullness*. 2nd ed. Downers Grove, Ill.: Inter-Varsity Press, 1979.

Wenward, Stephen F. *Fruit of the Spirit*. Leicester, England: Inter-Varsity Press, 1981.

Yoder, John H. "Discerning the Kingdom of God in the Struggles of the World." *International Review of Missions* 68 (1979).

Culture and Time

Claus, Tom, and Keitzman, Dale W., eds. *Christian Leadership in Indian America*. Chicago: Moody, 1976.

Frye, Jerry K. *Time: A Significant Variable of Intercultural Communication Research*. Armidale, Australia: Communication Association of the Pacific, 1980.

Hall, Edward T. *Beyond Culture*. Garden City, N.Y.: Anchor Books, 1976.

——————. *The Hidden Dimension*. Garden City, N.Y.: Doubleday, 1966.

——————. *The Silent Language*. Garden City, N.Y.: Doubleday, 1959.

Hallesby, Ole. *Temperament and the Christian Faith*. Minneapolis: Augsburg, 1962.

Hesselgrave, David J. *Communicating Christ Cross-Culturally*. Grand Rapids: Zondervan, 1978.

Koyama, Kosuke. *Three Mile an Hour God*. Maryknoll, N.Y.: Orbis, 1979.

La Haye, Tim. *Spirit-Controlled Temperament*. Wheaton: Tyndale House, 1966.

Mayers, Marvin K. *A Look at Latin American Lifestyles*. Dallas: SIL Museum of Anthropology, 1976.

Mayers, Marvin K. *Christianity Confronts Culture*. Grand Rapids: Zondervan, 1974.

Mbiti, John S. *New Testament Eschatology in an African Background*. London: Oxford University Press, 1971.

Moog, Vianna. *Bandeirantes e Pioneiros*. Rio de Janeiro: Editora Globo, 1954.

Nida, Eugene A. *Customs and Cultures*. New York: Harper and Row, 1954.

Sine, Tom. *The Mustard Seed Conspiracy.* Waco: Word, 1981.

Textor, Robert B., ed. *Cultural Frontiers of the Peace Corps.* Cambridge, Mass.: MIT Press, 1966.

Toffler, Alvin. *The Third Wave.* New York: Bantam Books, 1980.

Wright, Lawrence. *Clockwork Man: The Story of Time, Its Origins, Its Uses, Its Tyranny.* New York: Horizon Press, 1969.

Management and Time

Alexander, John W. *Managing Our Work.* Downers Grove, Ill.: InterVarsity Press, 1972.

Cohen, Peter. *The Gospel According to the Harvard Business School.* Garden City, N.Y.: Doubleday, 1973.

Davidson, Jim. *Effective Time Management.* New York: Human Sciences Press, 1978.

Dayton, Edward R. *God's Purpose/Man's Plans.* Monrovia, Calif.: World Vision, 1974.

DeBoer, John C. *How to Succeed in the Organization Jungle without Losing Your Religion.* Philadelphia: Pilgrim Press, 1972.

DeMoss, Arthur, and Enlow, David. *How to Change Your World in 12 Weeks.* Old Tappan, N.J.: Fleming H. Revell, 1969.

Drucker, Peter. *The Effective Executive.* New York: Harper and Row, 1967.

——————————. *Managing for Results.* New York: Harper and Row, 1964.

Engstrom, Ted W., and Dayton, Edward R. *The Art of Management for Christian Leaders.* Waco: Word, 1976.

Engstrom, Ted W., and Mackenzie, Alec. *Managing Your Time.* Grand Rapids: Zondervan, 1967.

Engstrom, Ted W., and Duroe, David J. *The Work Trap.* Old Tappan, N.J.: Fleming H. Revell, 1979.

Friesen, Garry, with Maxson, J. Robin. *Decision Making and the Will of God.* Portland: Multnomah Press, 1980.

Hendrix, Olan. *Management and the Christian Worker.* Rev. ed. Ft. Washington, Pa.: Christian Literature Crusade, 1972.

Hummel, Charles. *Tyranny of the Urgent.* Downers Grove, Ill.: InterVarsity Press, 1967.

King, Pat. *How to Have All the Time You Need Every Day.* Wheaton: Tyndale House, 1980.

Lakein, Alan. *How to Get Control of Your Time and Your Life.* New York: Peter H. Wyden, 1973.

Leas, Speed B. *Time Management.* Nashville: Abingdon, 1978.

Mackenzie, R. Alec. *The Time Trap.* New York: McGraw-Hill, 1972.

McCay, James T. *The Management of Time.* New York: Prentice-Hall, 1959.

DATE DUE

Ohmann, O. A. "Skyhooks: With Special Implications for Monday through Friday." *Harvard Business Review—On Management*. New York: Harper and Row, 1945.

Peterson, Eugene H. "The Unbusy Pastor." *Leadership* 2 (1981).

Shedd, Charlie W. *Time for All Things*. Nashville: Abingdon, 1962.

Sullivan, George. "Time: How They Squeeze the Most Out of It." *TWA Ambassador,* November 1977.

Trobisch, Walter. *Martin Luther's Quiet Time*. Downers Grove, Ill.: Inter-Varsity Press, 1975.

Webber, Ross A. *Time Is Money!* New York: The Free Press, 1980.

The Nature of Time

Custance, Arthur C. *Time and Eternity*. Grand Rapids: Zondervan, 1977.

Fraser, J. T., ed. *The Voices of Time*. New York: G. Braziller, 1966.

McIntire, C. T. "The Focus of Historical Study: A Christian View." *Fides et Historia* 14 (1981):6-17.

Priestley, J. B. *Man and Time*. London: Aldus Books, 1964.

Taylor, Mark C. "Time's Struggle with Space: Kierkegaard's Understanding of Temporality." *Harvard Theological Review* 66 (1973).

Whitrow, G. T. *The Nature of Time*. Baltimore: Penguin Books, 1975.

Yaker, Henri; Osmond, Humphrey; and Cheek, Frances, eds. *The Future of Time*. Garden City, N.Y.: Doubleday, 1971.